BECOMING
DIVERGENT

AN **UNOFFICIAL** BIOGRAPHY OF
SHAILENE WOODLEY AND **THEO JAMES**

BECOMING
DIVERGENT

AN **UNOFFICIAL** BIOGRAPHY OF
SHAILENE WOODLEY AND **THEO JAMES**

JOE ALLAN

MICHAEL O'MARA BOOKS LIMITED

First published in Great Britain in 2014 by
Michael O'Mara Books Limited
9 Lion Yard
Tremadoc Road
London SW4 7NQ

A CIP catalogue record for this book is available from the British Library.

Papers used by Michael O'Mara Books Limited are natural, recyclable products made
from wood grown in sustainable forests. The manufacturing processes conform to the
environmental regulations of the country of origin.

ISBN: 978-1-78243-212-8 in hardback print format
ISBN: 978-1-78243-213-5 in trade paperback format
ISBN: 978-1-78243-237-1 in e-book format

1 3 5 7 9 10 8 6 4 2

Designed and typeset by Design 23
Printed and bound by CPI Group (UK) Ltd, Croydon, CR0 4YY

www.mombooks.com

CONTENTS

Introduction

BECOMING DIVERGENT

VERONICA ROTH WAS BARELY OUT OF HER TEENS when she had the germ of an idea that would form the foundation for her first novel, *Divergent*. She says the book grew from a jumbled 'thought collage' that incorporated several random images: someone jumping from a tall building, a relentless, citywide, elevated train system and theories she had studied in her psychology classes. She had just finished her final year at Northwestern University when she signed the publishing deal that would culminate in *Divergent*'s extended run on *The New York Times* Best Seller list, and within a few months she landed the film rights deal that led to the book being adapted into the first of a potential trilogy of Hollywood movies.

Like many recent book-to-film adaptations, the novel sits comfortably alongside *The Hunger Games* and *Ender's Game* under the young adult banner, and has its roots in a well-established literary tradition: the 'coming of age' story. Whether it is Katniss

Everdeen in *The Hunger Games*, Holden Caulfield in *The Catcher in the Rye* or Harry Potter, what all of these stories have in common is a main character facing a life-changing event or important decision as they enter their late teens. They may be forced into situations over which they have no control and are often expected to make choices that have far-reaching effects on their families and the people they love. The main protagonist frequently discovers a previously hidden resourcefulness or overcomes his or her problems by forming an alliance or making a pact with others. Lessons learned on the hero's voyage of self-discovery invariably help him or her make choices that lead them to find their own way in the world, fulfil untapped potential and brings the realization that the answers to the important questions in life don't end in 'happy ever after'.

Divergent is no different. In Beatrice 'Tris' Prior, the book has a heroine who fits neatly into many of these formulas, but what sets *Divergent* apart from many of its contemporaries is the true to life nature of its main characters, ordinary people who are forced into extraordinary situations and are able to find the courage to become more than they were as their lives are thrown into chaos. There are no vampires, werewolves or genetically mutated super-heroes in the *Divergent* world. The great powers that bring great responsibility to Tris Prior are her innate intelligence, kindness and bravery, and it is these abilities she has to recognize and learn to use over the course of the story in order to deal with all that is thrown at her.

The action takes place in a future version of America, where civilization has broken down and rebuilt itself as a society divided into five separate factions. Each faction serves to reflect and uphold a different basic human characteristic: members of Dauntless are brave and fearless, Abnegation promotes selflessness and generosity, Amity encourages harmony and togetherness, Candor represents honesty and trustworthiness while Erudite values intelligence and learning above all else. At the age of sixteen, each child is given a test to see which faction they are most suited to joining, and on 'Choosing Day' they must decide themselves whether to stay with their birth faction or transfer to a new one. Leaving your birth faction means you are unlikely to see your parents or the rest of your family again.

Divergent's main themes deal with issues all teenagers experience: the realization that the choices we make as young adults will have a far-reaching effect on our lives, the anxiety that arises from breaking away from what our parents think is best for us, becoming who we truly want to be to achieve our personal goals in life and the ultimate conclusion that our parents will be there to support us no matter what we decide. As a main character, Tris Prior is instantly relatable. She is revealed to be Divergent – meaning she doesn't fit exclusively into just one faction – a displacement many young people will understand. The need to conform, to live by a set of rules or appear a certain way are all very common contemporary pressures that affect everyone, young and old. Tris, like many readers, has important life decisions to make while also dealing with the potential fallout that could arise from her choices. Added to that, she would meet a boy and fall in love for the first time.

The romance that weaves its way through the heart of the *Divergent* series is more straightforward than the complicated love lives of Katniss Everdeen, Peeta Mellark and Gale Hawthorne, the heroes of the *Hunger Games* trilogy, or Bella Swan, Edward Cullen and Jacob Black, the supernatural, star-crossed lovers central to Stephenie Meyer's *Twilight* saga. There are no messy love triangles for Tris Prior. She begins to fall in love with Tobias 'Four' Eaton from the moment she meets him. It's the simple, age-old story of girl meets boy, boy throws an enormous knife at girl, girl saves boy from a forcefully administered mind-control serum and, in between, there's a lot of jumping from incredibly fast moving trains, scaling tall buildings, heart-breaking personal sacrifice and then they all live happily ever after . . . we hope.

The two actors who bring these lovers to life in the film version of *Divergent* are Shailene Woodley and Theo James. Like their characters growing up in opposing factions of the *Divergent* world, their separate journeys to the big screen adaptation of the book couldn't be more different – one is a seasoned veteran with over fifteen years' experience in the US television and film industry, the other is a relative newcomer who stumbled into acting on a whim. One was born and raised in a peaceful suburb of sunny California in the USA, while the other grew up in a not quite so sunny corner of England.

For Shailene, it would seem her fate was sealed very early. She had chosen acting as something that would dominate her whole life when she was little more than a child. The numerous television and movie sets on which she spent her formative years and early teens would become her playground and her classroom. Subsequently, her formal education had to fit in with her busy working schedule, while Theo had been lucky enough to attend one of the most respected boys' schools in England and had even gained a university degree before he had to make any final choices about his long-term future. Theo made the decision that acting would be something to consider pursuing as a 'proper' career well into his adult life.

What they do have in common, and what they have both shown in their careers to date, is an unwavering commitment to their work, an instinct to fiercely protect their own individuality, a unique perspective on fame and how to use it as a positive force for change, as well as a deeper understanding of who they are and their place in the world. These are all qualities that set them apart from most of their contemporaries, making them stand out from the pack. Qualities that make them hard to define and categorize, and, it could be argued, which make them perfectly suited to becoming Divergent.

Chapter One

SHAILENE: CALIFORNIA DREAMER

SHAILENE DIANN WOODLEY WAS BORN on 15 November 1991 to father, Lonnie, a school principle, and mother, Lori, a guidance counsellor working for several schools in the Simi Valley area of southern California. Shailene is descended from an unusually long, unbroken line of five generations of California natives with direct links back to the American Gold Rush.

Shailene's unique name can be attributed to her mother, Lori, who, at the age of eighteen, was sitting in her car in a traffic jam when she saw the word 'Shai' on the number plate of the vehicle in front. She thought it would make a good nickname and began adding various endings to it until she came up with Shailene as a full name. Shai would become the affectionate family nickname for her daughter and the one Shailene would later insist her closest friends use instead of her full name.

Shailene was their first child and, as such, she was delivered into a very loving, attentive and stable home environment. It could be said that Shailene's parents were a fairly ordinary couple; they certainly had no strong links to the film and television world that would eventually become so important in their daughter's life, as close as they lived to Hollywood's bright lights.

Simi Valley, in contrast, is a peaceful, rural area of southern California, almost completely enclosed by the Santa Susanna mountain range and the Simi Hills. It sits just over thirty miles – and a half-hour drive – from the considerably harsher and more bustling environment of downtown Los Angeles. It is a fairly affluent, middle-class area of America. Less than eight per cent of households could be considered to be living below the poverty line (as opposed to the average of sixteen per cent for the USA as a whole) and it was voted America's fifth 'happiest city' in a 2013 survey. Known by most Americans as the site of the Ronald Reagan Presidential Library (where the former President was laid to rest after his death in 2004), or the location chosen for the infamous Rodney King trial in 1991 – where the local jury's decision to acquit the LA police officers involved in a suspected racial attack caused riots that spread across much of America in 1992 – but to the rest of us, we probably know it best as the location used for filming most of the exterior scenes in the television series *Little House on the Prairie*. The Valley's biggest employer is the Bank of America, which has a workforce of nearly four thousand staff at its corporate headquarters. The other main industries located in the region produce heavy machinery, tools and metals.

The summers are long, with the lucky residents enjoying an average six months of unbroken sunshine weather (above 25°C) from May to October. Aside from the obvious threat of earthquakes that exists throughout the state of California, Simi Valley's biggest problem is wildfires. Long periods of temperatures in the high thirties create a lethal combination of dry grasslands and low humidity, which erupts into deadly, out-of-control wildfires every few years. Surrounded by two vast mountain ranges and set in an expanse of open country that includes over twenty city parks, there is ample opportunity for the pursuit of many outdoor activities. Aside from its six golf courses, there are multiple hiking and cycling trails as well as facilities for mountain biking and horse riding. It's no wonder Shailene would grow up loving nature and playing in the open air. It was literally on her doorstep every day.

Shailene was considered a very normal, happy and affectionate child. Confident and outgoing, she made friends easily and spent most of her time playing with the other neighbourhood kids her own age. Although she was more of an outdoors kind of girl, Shailene, like most young people, started watching movies and television with her friends and she vividly remembers *Beauty and the Beast* as the first film she saw at the age of three. She has also spoken about her love of other Disney classics, *The Little Mermaid* and *Pocahontas*. When Shailene was about to turn three, the Woodley family expanded with the birth of her brother Tanner. He immediately became a much-cherished addition to the household and was a constant playmate for Shailene growing up. She was understandably protective of her little brother and they maintain a very strong bond to this day. The Woodleys had become a tight-knit family unit of four, and they quickly settled into a fairly ordinary, contented existence. Over the next few years, however, things were about to happen in Shailene's life that would change it forever.

Shailene's move into the spotlight began very early. She was a very pretty little girl, with arresting hazel eyes, but there was something else about her – she had something special. From the age of four she was attracting enough attention to be offered numerous child modelling jobs in her local area. People commented on the fact that she had a very relatable, down-to-earth quality and that she seemed to have a real talent for the work. It wasn't long before these modelling jobs became a large part of her young life. Given all the attention she was getting at such a young age, it's no surprise she soon expressed an interest in acting – not as a career, but as a hobby. She told *Girls' Life*, 'I tried gymnastics and that was fun, but I wanted to try something different.'

She asked her parents if she could sign up for some theatre acting classes and it was there she was spotted by an agent. Her parents' lack of any grand plan, in terms of their daughter's acting career, at least, is best illustrated by a story Shailene told *W* magazine: 'An agent called, and my mom was like, "What's an agent?"' It's clear that Lori Woodley definitely couldn't be described as a typical 'stage mom'. Lori told the *Ventura County Star* she compared the experience of sending her daughter to those early auditions as being like 'the first time you put your child in a swimming pool', but she explained things had worked out fine and believed that in some ways it was better they had gone into it with no prior film industry knowledge. At least that meant they had no unrealistic expectations or ulterior motives regarding their daughter's career. It would seem their ambitions for her were refreshingly simple – Shailene told the *Hollywood Reporter* that her mother had laid down three simple rules she had to follow: 'Stay the person I knew I was, do well in school and have fun. If I did all those things, I could continue to act.'

Shailene was soon being placed on casting lists all over Los Angeles as her newly hired agent set to work. Once this treadmill was set in motion, it quickly turned into a steady stream of television commercials and small acting roles. She told *New York* magazine about her first job: 'I believe it was a Kellogg's commercial,' she recalled. 'I did over forty, forty-five commercials when I was younger . . . from the age of probably six-and-a-half.' As the work poured in, Shailene was getting busier and busier and the jobs were coming from further afield.

Shailene was now attending Township Elementary School in Simi Valley and was trying to maintain all her normal school activities, keep up with her homework and make time for her friends. Everyone adapted quickly to this unusual arrangement and soon the whole Woodley family began pitching in to help keep everything running smoothly. Instead of dropping their daughter off at cheerleading rehearsals or soccer practice, they were taking her to modelling or acting jobs in the city and, for several years, driving her to and from auditions became the norm.

Shailene emphasized this sense of ordinariness in her early life, and how acting fitted into it, when she told the *Boston Phoenix*, 'It was never the typical child actor situation. I went to school, got picked up, went to an audition, came home and played with my friends. When I was at the auditions, my friends were at soccer practice, then we'd reconvene in the neighbourhood park.' She explained this as a 'secret life', saying, 'If I booked a commercial or something when I was younger I never told my friends. Three quarters of my friends didn't even know I acted until [third] year of high school. I never talked about it. It was fun for me, but it was never something like, 'Oh, guys, I'm an actor . . . '

Everyone else in the family shared this view and considered it to be mostly an 'after-school hobby', and it soon became an everyday, if unusual, part of Shailene's childhood. In an interview with the *Los Angeles Times*, she recalled that as time went on she continued to strive for a 'normal', well-rounded and fulfilled childhood. 'I'd do classes for a year, then take a year off to do other things – build tables or climb mountains.'

The southern California landscape that was her childhood home is famous for its natural beauty. Growing up in a green belt region, surrounded by a landscape filled with mountains, trees, rivers and lakes, it's no wonder Shailene would develop a lifelong interest in environmental issues. She told 411Mania.com, 'Anything that has to do with nature, I'm all there. I love the outdoors.'

She has often talked about her love of playing in the open air, even joking to *Marie Claire* magazine that her long 'monkey toes' were a huge asset when climbing trees barefoot as a child. She would also go swimming with her mother, Lori. She told the *Hollywood Reporter*, 'I'm really comfortable in the water – I was born in the water, started swimming at one-and-a-half, so the water's always been [my] safe zone.' Her mother would later describe her daughter in the *Ventura County Star* as 'compassionate, loving and adventurous . . . not an indoors, sit-around-the-TV type.'

By the time her seventh birthday came around, Shailene's career was really starting to take off and she had been cast in the TV movie *Replacing Dad*. This was to be her first major television role and the first chance for the wider television and film industry to see her in action. Although it was not a big part, or a high profile project, it was a major step up for Shailene and served as a signal that she was now moving away from modelling and commercials and was looking to start a real acting career.

It worked, and offers of more acting work started to come in thick and fast. Although she was still not one-hundred per cent committed to life as a child actor, she happily took the jobs which really interested her and passed on the ones that didn't.

She further stressed her on–off relationship with the job to the *Boston Phoenix*: 'I didn't [take any acting jobs] for a while, to maybe eight? Nine? And from there I started doing small co-star roles on TV and then guest star roles.' One week she would turn up in a recurring role in Washington D.C.-set crime drama, *The District*, playing the daughter of one of the main police detectives and the next she would get a one-off gig as the younger, flashback version of a runaway mental patient in missing person drama, *Without a Trace*. Around this time she had also managed to carve out an interesting niche for herself playing, in several flash back episodes, the younger version of Jordan Cavanaugh (the main character portrayed by Jill Hennessy) in forensic detective drama, *Crossing Jordan*.

In 2003, at the age of eleven, Shailene landed the role of Kaitlin Cooper, younger sister of main character Marissa Cooper (as portrayed by Mischa Barton) on *The O.C.* Set in the waterfront community of Newport Beach, in Orange County, California, the show focused on the lives (and loves) of a group of spoilt, super-rich teenagers and their even richer, even more spoilt parents.

The show had launched on the Fox Network to surprisingly high ratings, and was set to become one of the most talked about, and critically acclaimed, dramas of 2003–04. A real pop culture phenomenon, the show would change how American television executives thought about programming for teenagers, and young women in particular. This mini-revolution would spark the creation of a huge number of roles for young actresses in female-oriented shows such as *Ugly Betty*, *Gossip Girl*, *Pretty Little Liars* and, eventually, the show that would soon play a major part in changing Shailene's life forever – *The Secret Life of the American Teenager*.

Kaitlin (Shailene's character in *The O.C.*) spent most of her time on the show off-camera, at boarding school. So although this was a prominent recurring role, Shailene only appeared on screen as Kaitlin in six episodes. When the show returned for season two, Kaitlin had been re-cast and was now played by Willa Holland. This was Shailene's first experience of the harsher elements of the industry and a valuable lesson, she explained to Moviefone.com: 'I was eleven when they decided to bring her back . . . they actually re-auditioned me . . . At eleven, I was like a little mouse child. I looked like an eight-year-old. That same year I filmed a movie in which I played a nine-year-old.' She dismissed any feelings of disappointment with a laugh, 'I didn't go through puberty until late. I was the fifteen-year-old who had no boobs ... there was no weirdness when Willa Holland got it because she was so obviously right for the role . . . and I was so obviously not.'

This was a gracious response to something that must have been difficult to deal with for one so young, but some might say she had a lucky escape. In the show's fourth season, Kaitlin (now played by Willa Holland) went on to date another character played by infamous bad-boy music star, Chris Brown, known for his often fraught relationship with popstar Rihanna.

She looked back fondly on her time on the show, telling 411Mania.com, 'I did *The O.C.* at a very young age . . . everyone was very sweet and everyone was so excited about the show. I'm definitely glad I had that experience . . . it was cool to say that I was on *The O.C.* the first season.'

One-off appearances continued on shows like the number-one-rated comedy *Everybody Loves Raymond* (as the charmingly named 'Snotty Girl'), *My Name is Earl*, *Cold Case*, *CSI: New York* and in television movies such as *A Place Called Home*, *Once Upon a*

Mattress, *Final Approach* and *Felicity: An American Girl Adventure*. It was the latter that would be Shailene's most high profile job to date.

Felicity was based on a character featured in the extremely popular (and seemingly endless) *American Girl* series of books, which are aimed squarely at pre-teen girls. The series was famous for its plucky heroines who embarked on daring and exciting adventures, set against real events from American history. The film takes place in Williamsburg, Virginia during the onset of the American Revolution. It would be a perfect showcase for the blossoming Shailene, who, by now, was on the adventure of a lifetime herself. Looking back at her thirteen-year-old self, Shailene was quick to recognize the spirit of adventure and self-sufficient streak she shared with the character, telling 411Mania. com, '[Felicity] was so similar to me. She was a go-getter, she was independent and she fought for what she wanted without being rude about it. And that's definitely how I was growing up.' Giving further insight into her own character, she continued, 'I've always dreamed about driving and then moving out, and I've always been an independent person who still loves their family, which I think is a very hard balance to find, but I think I find that balance.'

Although she was now living a very busy, charmed life, balancing school and her ever-increasing work commitments, Shailene was never happier than when she was at home, spending time with her friends and family. If they weren't outside swimming or hiking, they would be doing something creative. She especially liked sewing. They would spend hours making things and doing arts and crafts together. In school she described herself as 'outgoing and extrovert', telling *Girls' Life* she was a 'really good student; I always got straight As. My favourite subject was biology, and it seemed I was involved in everything.' She took part in several extra-curricular school activities including leader of the Pep Rally (an event that took place before school sports events to generate excitement and build team spirit) and the school student council; she even described herself as a 'choir geek'. She was definitely someone who liked to be at the centre of everything. She continued, 'I loved school and the social aspect of it.'

What she wasn't so keen on, and made every effort to avoid, were the cliques. The talking behind people's backs and gossip that tended to rule the halls and classrooms of the average American school were not something she was interested in being a part of. 'I can't stand drama! I think it's ridiculous. Honestly, I was the girl who – the second drama came up – would get up and leave.'

Shailene, like most girls her age, was also having her first experiences of dating. She had a fairly sober and sensible approach to the whole situation. She told SheReality.com, 'I think a lot of high school relationships are [immature]. I've had a couple of those where you're in the moment and you think that he could be the one and everything's fine, and then two weeks later he does something stupid and you're like, okay, next.'

On the whole, she was juggling all the elements of her relatively complicated life with amazing ease. She compared it to playing a strategic board game: 'You're kind of going through each different aspect of your life and you're testing the waters . . . it's a fun, exciting time, but I also think you have to be careful . . . when you're in the moment, it could seem one way, but when you look at the big picture from afar, it's completely different.'

This picture of her relatively carefree outlook was confirmed in an interview with the *Huffington Post* when she stated: 'I am the happiest person, literally, I am annoyingly happy to some people.

I was naturally born an optimist; I love life, even when things are not going so great.' That positive outlook was about to be seriously tested by the events unfolding in her personal life.

Shailene was in her freshman (first) year at high school when her seemingly secure home life took an unexpected turn: her parents decided to split up. Looking back on this troubled time in an interview with *Girls' Life*, she described her parents' divorce as 'healthy' and 'for the better'. Recalling how it caused further personal complications, she said, 'It was tough [moving into] a new house and balancing high school, friends, boys and everything.' She went on to say, 'You have to stay strong and realize that it's not affecting just your life, but the entire family's life and everything else, too.' She later told HollywoodChicago.com, 'I'm a firm believer in when something challenging occurs in life, you go through that dark low. And when you're at that low, something will inspire you.' She stressed her positive attitude about the situation by saying, 'I think it takes getting to a low point in life to get to a high place and [to then get to] where you [want to] be in the future.'

It certainly was a challenge for everyone in the Woodley household. They had relocated to nearby Palmdale a few years earlier, so it was with mixed emotions she moved to another new home, back in Simi Valley, with her mother and younger brother. The whole family rallied to keep things as stable as possible. The family unit may have appeared to break apart, but life went on as normal for Shailene and Tanner, and every effort was being made to maintain continuity in the children's education and after-school activities. Shailene explained to HollywoodChicago.com that she thought this unconventional situation was nothing out of the ordinary: 'I think that a lot of families are that way, whether people like to admit it or not; every family has a dysfunction.

It's not a bad thing at all, it's just life's journey.' Both her parents remained a constant, and encouraging, presence and Shailene was keen to downplay the impact of the change of circumstances on her ever-complicated work–home life, telling SheReality.com, 'It's a very interesting dynamic, but other than that life has just been the same. I've stayed with the same friends and have the most amazing family ever, so I've been very lucky.' The truth was she would need all the support they had to offer to help her overcome the next challenge that was about to come her way.

As she entered her sophomore (second) year at high school, Shailene was diagnosed with scoliosis. Shailene told the WebMD website, 'We were getting ready to go swimming and I was in a bikini. My best friend was like, "Shai, your spine is weird."' With scoliosis, the spine can look like an 'S' or a 'C' from behind. A trip to her doctor confirmed there was a problem, but her diagnosis was relatively good. Identified as idiopathic scoliosis, Shailene had the most common form of the condition. Although in typical cases the cause of the disease is unknown, it often occurs during puberty and early adolescence and can cause extreme curvature of the spine. While it can become crippling and painful if a severe case goes undetected, it is curable via an operation or, in the case of younger patients such as Shailene where their bones are still growing, with the use of a body brace. Thankfully, she was just under the forty-five degree curvature tipping point that would have meant she would be recommended for surgery. So instead, for the foreseeable future, Shailene would have to wear a customized chest-to-hip plastic body brace. Fortunately, she was able to take the brace off when she was swimming, out socializing with friends or when she was working, but otherwise she wore it for eighteen hours every day for the next two years.

Remembering these difficult times, she told WebMD.com, 'I laugh under pressure, so I was okay. It wasn't until the fourth week of wearing a brace that I said, "Whoa, this is a bummer."' She went on to explain that despite the inconvenience and discomfort, 'It's like braces in your mouth. You go in and get it tightened and it hurts for a while.' It is testament to Shailene's strength of character and typically positive nature that she refused to let her disability become a burden or a hindrance.

In the end, the treatment was completely successful, and in December 2008 Shailene was given the good news that she didn't have to wear the brace anymore. She told MoviesOnline.ca about her ongoing relationship with the disease, explaining, 'I still have scoliosis but it was never a question of whether I could be active or not . . . it's not something that will ever affect [my life] . . . Every now and then you get a little bit of pain, but everyone has their stuff to deal with . . . but it's never been physically limiting at all.' She wanted to stress she, like most other sufferers, was capable of living a normal life and was determined not to let the disease change her future plans. 'You can still get pregnant . . . you can bungee jump. You can skydive. It does not hold you back from anything.'

As if to prove a point, she took a part-time job working in a local paint store and learned to drive as soon as she passed the US legal driving age of sixteen. She had earned enough money from babysitting jobs to buy a car, but knew she was not going to get anything too fancy. As luck would have it, her aunt was looking to sell her old Toyota Prius and gave it to Shailene for the same price as a Honda she had been thinking of buying. Considered the most environmentally friendly car on the market, the Prius, with her ongoing and ever-growing interest in preserving the environment, was the perfect car for Shailene. However, taking to the roads proved to be eventful, as she admitted to *Marie Claire*, with a degree of embarrassment, that she'd been handed a speeding ticket within a matter of months. She learned her lesson fast and has been a more conscientious driver ever since.

Entering her teenage years, it was obvious Shailene was growing up to be a very well-rounded young woman. Despite her acting hobby, she had managed to keep her feet on the ground and was interested in the same things as most people her age. She has described herself as a 'total dork' on several occasions, admitting she has a tendency to be clumsy and uncoordinated. She wasn't exactly tall for her age at five feet eight inches, but she has long legs for her height and because she is not too skinny, she appears strong and athletic. Even with her scoliosis, she has the look of a cheerleader, but chose not to pursue the hobby as her other interests meant she was always on the move. If it wasn't an audition, an acting class or a job, she was taking part in some outdoor activity – hiking, swimming or climbing – Shailene has turned up to several press interviews with scratches on her hands and arms, which she explains as an unavoidable consequence of her 'rough and tumble' outdoor pursuits.

She also developed an interest in music – listening, rather than playing – specifically to indie rock. She states her favourite bands as The Hush Sound, Bon Iver, Radiohead and Foo Fighters.

Shailene would never consider herself a movie buff, however; she was far too much of an outdoor girl for that. She told *Entertainment Weekly*, 'Some movies have made me cry; some movies have made me laugh, but I've never thought, "Wow – if it weren't for that movie, I'd be a different person."' When asked to name a film that had affected her emotionally, more than just as entertainment, she mentioned Disney's *Pocahontas*. 'If you listen to the lyrics, they actually have incredibly valuable lessons for human beings to learn, and whenever I need a pick-me-up, I just watch *Pocahontas*.'

She remained respectful and grateful to her parents for the sacrifices they made when she was growing up and this is best exemplified by the fact that she says whenever she is away from home, she won't go to sleep without texting her parents 'Goodnight'.

What starts to emerge is the picture of a well-adjusted, confident sixteen-year-old girl, but Shailene was quick to point out that, like most adolescents, she had her periods of rebellion and angst.

In an interview with SheReality.com she said, 'I think that all teenage girls kind of go through that mean stage where the world revolves around them.' She elaborated on this when talking to Collider.com: 'People who are like, "No, I had the perfect adolescence" make me wonder how that is possible.' Shailene revealed her own dark period was when she was fourteen or fifteen. 'I was never very rebellious. I never did things to rebel against society, or against my parents, but I did think I knew everything . . . Then, one day, I woke up and realized I was a dot in the universe and that quickly dissipated.' Surprising maturity for one so young.

Perhaps it is this realization – along with the lyrics to *Pocahontas*'s theme 'Colours of the Wind' ringing in her ears – that might explain Shailene's growing interest and involvement with recycling, preservation, nutrition and broader environmental issues.

Lots of teenagers experiment with vegetarianism and

experience increased social awareness, but Shailene was embarking on something that would become a lifelong passion, an involvement with causes and ideals that she would continue to support and champion into her adult life.

This is some of what sets Shailene apart. She is far from the self-obsessed, self-important image of the average adolescent (not to mention the average adolescent actress); her lifelong love of the outdoors and respect for nature were becoming a unique foundation on which she was building interests that covered a multitude of different environmental issues and self-improvement ideas. She started to read books about herbalism – the study of plants and their medicinal and nutritional purposes – and indigenous tribes in far-flung countries, eager to learn how other societies flourished and respected the ecosystem of the world they lived in.

Always keen to stress she still considered acting to be a constant and fun part of her life, she wanted everyone to know her education and growth as a young woman were more important. She rated learning at school and ongoing self-education as the most important 'habits' that any young person could pick up. She saw herself as a 'knowledge sponge' and was adamant the most important lessons in life came from life itself. Only by becoming comfortable in your own skin, achieving personal awareness and pushing yourself to appreciate and accept other cultures could you fully understand your own place in the world. She told HollywoodChicago.com: 'I've taken acting classes my whole life, and I always say I've never learned anything about acting in acting classes, but I've learned more about myself than I could ever imagine.'

It had been a truly eventful few years. Forced to show extreme bravery and maturity during some difficult personal situations, as well as experiencing some real career highs, she had become hungry for knowledge and self-improvement, as well as realizing the need to educate others. She was truly showing her own Divergent nature. It was armed with a newfound confidence and willingness to accept a challenge that Shailene would embark on the next important phase of her acting career.

Chapter Two

THEO: MEET THE TALL, DARK STRANGER

THEO JAMES WAS BORN IN OXFORD on 16 December 1984. His birth name was Theodore Peter James Kenneth Taptiklis, which gives an accurate, if slightly confusing, signal of his complicated family tree.

His real surname is a remnant of his Greek ancestry. His grandfather had been born and raised in Greece but left as a young man and settled in New Zealand. He met and married a local woman and eventually Theo's father, Philip, was born. The whole family were soon on the move again. They emigrated, this time travelling to the other side of the world, settling in England. Here the family put down roots and began to flourish.

Theo's mother, Jane, was born in Cambridge, and her mother was born and raised in Scotland. In an interview with the *Toronto Star*, Theo jokingly described the Taptiklis clan as 'a Greek, Scottish, Kiwi family who lived on a goose farm in north-west London.'

Philip and Jane married in 1973 and it wasn't long before

they started a family, with Emmeline Lucinda Taptiklis arriving in 1974. Over the next few years the Taptiklis household expanded further with the birth of Theo's two brothers and another sister. Theo's position in the family line-up was set. 'I was the youngest of five kids, which meant I always had to fight for attention and I was always put in my place, two things that are very useful to remember now.'

Theo had a very normal, middle-class upbringing and both of his parents worked in secure, professional positions and, as such, the family led comfortable and contented lives. Money wasn't tight, but with a house full of children, Theo's parents had to work for everything they needed. Theo is quoted as saying he is extremely grateful for the many sacrifices his parents made to ensure he, and all of his brothers and sisters, had a great start in life. They have been a constant support, always available to offer advice and give their opinions while he was making up his mind about which career path he would take and, most of all, to help him keep his feet on the ground when he eventually achieved a level of success. He recalled with a laugh, 'To this day, if I ever started becoming a prima donna, I'm sure I would get soundly slapped in the face by all of them.' In reality, as the youngest, Theo did get plenty of attention, both from his parents and his older siblings, but he could never be described as spoilt.

The family had settled in the Princes Risborough region of Buckinghamshire, a few miles from Aylesbury in the south-east of England. A much sought-after property location with a very friendly atmosphere, it is a peaceful, rural spot that plays host to a weekly farmers' market. In all, it was a fairly idyllic place to grow up.

Theo attended a local primary school and then, due to his

above average exam results, was eligible to apply to Aylesbury Grammar School. Aylesbury is a boys-only state secondary school that is open to everyone, but has a very selective, academic-based intake policy. Considered one of the best schools in the country, it offers a well-rounded and traditional education, as well as encouraging more creative activities seen as necessary for a solid grounding in life. It has gained an exceptional reputation in the areas of technology, science, languages, maths and computing.

Like most all-boys schools of this type, sports are an important part of the curriculum and Theo was keen to get involved. He took boxing lessons and, although it wasn't something he was fanatical about at the time, he would take it up again when he was at university and incorporated it as an important element of his normal fitness routine.

In an interview with Upcoming-movies.com, Theo describes how he started sparring regularly with an old friend. These sessions became so intense that on one occasion he accidentally dislocated his shoulder during a match – such dedication would certainly come in very handy during the extensive *Divergent* training that was just around the corner.

The school likes to support and develop creativity among its pupils and encourages them to get involved in all areas of the performing arts, including the orchestra, singing, dance and theatre, as well as day trips to see plays, musicals and concerts with the girls from the neighbouring, all-female, branch of the school. Strangely, at this stage, Theo didn't take full advantage of the opportunities that were coming his way, stating he was not particularly interested in acting at all: 'I did my share of kid acting, like lots of us do. I even played King Herod when I was six, but when I got to the end of my school period, that was it.'

As his parents had no real links to the entertainment industry or the acting profession, there was no pressure from them to follow this path and he had not developed any particular interest or inclination to pursue acting as a hobby, let alone as a potential career. He told Variety.com that he felt he wasn't emotionally ready to go straight from school to fully committing to acting as a profession, saying, 'It might have worked for others, but I was not mature enough to do it.' He believed he lacked the necessary life experience, suggesting he 'needed to be a bit more grounded and to have more to draw from.' He concluded: 'It was the right decision for me.'

Acting was definitely not on Theo's radar at that point; that bug would not bite him until he had finished his studies at university. 'I thought about every career possible, from being a speech therapist to a pub owner. They all had their appeal.'

Theo may not have made up his mind about a future career, but he was becoming a well-rounded, educated and active young man. He had always looked after himself and aside from boxing and an interest in general fitness, Theo was a keen swimmer and liked free-diving, the sport of underwater diving that relies on the individual's ability to hold their breath until resurfacing. As he grew older he would also become a keen scuba diver. He took several part-time and temporary jobs to help make ends meet – including as a lifeguard, bar worker, even cleaning jobs within the NHS.

It was during this seemingly aimless time that Theo developed a love for playing music. He told the *Toronto Star*, 'Music became a very big thing in my life,' and this obsession would grow as he started playing and singing in various bands. Aside from his singing voice, Theo was now a fairly proficient piano and guitar player – with a little harmonica thrown in for good measure.

After achieving solid exam results at Aylesbury, Theo was offered a place at the University of Nottingham. After a three-year course and a lot of hard work, in 2006 he completed his degree in philosophy. He had more or less stumbled into studying this subject, conceiving an interest in philosophy and assuming he would enjoy exploring the area further. In the end, it failed to capture his imagination and he acknowledged the ideas and theories behind the subject interested him a lot more than the actual studying of it did. 'I thought that was going to be the big thing for me, I really did,' he said. 'But, after a while, I found it all a bit disappointing. I loved ethics, but logic was the bane of my existence. I remember one exam when I only got ten out of a hundred.' He finished: 'I realized that I would probably be screwed if I seriously continued to pursue philosophy on an academic level, so I dropped it.'

It is obvious that at this point, Theo was slightly unsure of where he was going in life and had yet to find a passion outside of music that really grabbed him and pointed to something he could continue as a career. He thought about studying law, but worried it would take too long, saying, 'I was way too impatient for that.' He graduated instead without taking Honours and left university in the same position as many young graduates: with a degree he had no intention of using to find a job.

It was a bizarre twist of fate that then led him to the next step on his road to acting and a place at the prestigious Bristol Old Vic Theatre School. With a smile he told the *Toronto Star*, 'I'm almost ashamed to tell you [how it happened],' before revealing that, 'My girlfriend at the time was auditioning for drama school, so I decided to apply along with her just for a lark.' It's unlikely there was the same light-hearted atmosphere back at home that night when, in the end, he got a place and she didn't. Theo's fate was unexpectedly sealed. This was the opportunity of a lifetime and would finally steer him towards acting as a full-time career.

Founded in 1946 as an offshoot from the Bristol Old Vic Theatre Company, the school was seen, primarily, as a training ground for young stage actors. Although it was, even in its formative years, a highly respected and popular theatre company, the Bristol Old Vic suffered the same financial hardships as everyone else in the years following the Second World War. It was only after an extremely popular musical production transferred from the Bristol Old Vic to London's West End, and the substantial profits that were ploughed back into the theatre and the school, that it began to flourish.

The school runs a variety of courses offering qualifications in all areas of film, television, radio and theatre. These include behind-the-scenes roles, covering all aspects of production, design, business and management, as well as acting. The acting course is considered to be one of the most prestigious in the UK as it only accepts twelve students per year – from over 2,500 applicants. Some of its most famous graduates include Oscar winners Daniel Day-Lewis and Jeremy Irons, recent Bond girl Naomie Harris, *X-Men*'s Patrick Stewart and *Blackadder*'s Miranda Richardson.

Theo was accepted into the school with a view to becoming a stage actor and he remembers his time there very fondly. Suddenly he had a purpose, and for the first time in his life a clear view of what his future could be. In an interview with the *Toronto Star*, he recalled, 'The Bristol Old Vic is great; it's a very classical school and that's just what I needed.' He went on to say, 'The discipline was eye-opening. I finally came up against people who wouldn't take my indecisiveness anymore and they kicked me into shape.' At last, he had found a passion that truly gripped him and propelled him forward, a subject that could help him channel his obvious intellect, creativity and energy into something positive.

In early 2007, Theo was cast in a production of Edward Albee's *The Zoo Story*, which was set to run for four performances at Nottingham's New Theatre. It is a one-act play featuring only two characters, Jerry and Peter. Theo was cast as Peter and received great praise from the play's director, Charlie Brafman, who wrote on his blog: 'He was the only actor [of a young age] who I knew could bring a suitable gravitas to a performance, in which he played against his typical casting with great sensitivity.' The Nottingham University Student Union magazine, *Impact*, described the play as, 'Twanging with tension from the start, this is a production that will reel you in so close that its explosive finale will have you picking shrapnel from your skin on the way out of the auditorium.'

Over the course of the next three years, Theo would appear in at least two productions of an eclectic mix of plays per year, including as Larry in Patrick Marber's *Closer* – the role played by Clive Owen in the 2004 film adaptation – the Prince of Verona in Shakespeare's *Romeo and Juliet*, Algernon Moncrieff in Oscar Wilde's *The Importance of Being Ernest*, Abanazar in *Aladdin*, as well as parts in lesser known plays such as *Gizmo Love*, *Machinal* and *The Slippery Soapbox*.

Theo remembers one performance in particular that changed the course of his career. He had been cast as Stanley Kowalski in the theatre school production of Tennessee Williams' *A Streetcar Named Desire* and he watched the legendary 1951 film version starring Marlon Brando in the role as research. He recalled: 'That did it for me. Instantly! I saw that an actor could be almost animal and yet very human as well,' adding, 'Brando looked so cool and masculine, but he also showed me that vulnerability could be a powerful tool.' It was a lesson he obviously never forgot, as it was these very qualities that first grabbed the attention of the *Divergent* production team and Veronica Roth, and eventually landed him the role of a certain Tobias 'Four' Eaton.

As Theo entered his late teens and early twenties, he began to grow into his looks, filling out his rather lanky six-foot frame. Now more lean and athletic, his deep-set, dark brown eyes, defined cheek bones and full lips ensured his appearance would set him apart from the crowd and would make a lasting impression on casting directors and audiences alike. Theo wasn't particularly conscious of how he looked, which gave him an easy and masculine charm – perfect for the romantic leading men roles his Mediterranean good looks were obviously going to bring his way.

In 2009, his final year at the Old Vic, he auditioned for a part in Woody Allen's London-based film, *You Will Meet a Tall Dark Stranger*. It was a small speaking role, so it seems likely Allen was involved in Theo's actual casting, and there is no doubt the experience of working on this production and in such esteemed company would be invaluable to Theo in the future, as he told Variety.com. 'Working with Woody Allen was extremely gratifying . . . He has such a vast catalogue of great work that doing one of his films was somewhat unreal.' The film was to be the last of Woody's recent films set in the UK, following *Match Point*, *Scoop* and *Cassandra's Dream*.

You Will Meet a Tall Dark Stranger saw Woody briefly return to a British setting after he had already started his mini-tour of Europe with *Vicky Cristina Barcelona*. He would continue this European run with *To Rome with Love* and, with what would become his biggest box-office hit to date, *Midnight in Paris*.

On set, Theo had the chance to rub shoulders with some real Hollywood heavyweights, including the stars of the film, Antonio Banderas, Naomi Watts and Josh Brolin, as well as the opportunity to share the screen with some very well-respected home-grown talents such as Freida Pinto, Ewen Bremner, Anna Friel, Philip Glenister, Celia Imrie and Pauline Collins. Not a bad start for someone who hadn't even graduated from drama school yet!

Theo was particularly excited to meet one man appearing in the film, Sir Anthony Hopkins, and their encounter would leave a lasting impression on the young actor. Hopkins had become a major Hollywood star after his performance as serial killer Hannibal Lecter in *The Silence of the Lambs* won him the Oscar for Best Actor in 1991. But the story of his career prior to this success was a rollercoaster of highs and lows that had taken him from working alongside some of the most esteemed directors in Hollywood – such as Michael Cimino, Richard Attenborough and David Lynch – to a string of made-for-television films including an adaptation of Jackie Collins' *Hollywood Wives* alongside a cast of US television has-beens.

In *You Will Meet a Tall Dark Stranger*, Hopkins plays an old man, Alfie, who, after a mid-life crisis, has left his wife and re-married a much younger, gold-digging woman, Charmaine. Theo's character, Ray, is the young, fit, roguish charmer who seduces Charmaine and begins an affair with her. Theo gets the chance to show off some serious muscles and his encounters with Charmaine are extremely flirtatious. He also has two scenes with Hopkins himself, one involving a brutal fist-fight. Working closely on these scenes allowed the pair to spend time together, with Hopkins giving Theo some valuable advice. Hopkins was at pains to point out that every young actor should be aware that making films can be exciting and deeply satisfying, but it should also be seen as a means to an end. Theo explained to Variety.com that 'he's very real about the industry,' recalling Hopkins had insisted that being an actor is the same as any other profession, saying, 'It is an art form . . . but it is also a job.' Theo spent many hours soaking up the great man's stories and he would get some important lessons about the business he was entering.

Theo's first role after graduating that year was appearing in a film produced by *Star Wars* creator, George Lucas. The film was a Second World War drama based on true events entitled *Red Tails*, which told the story of the all-African-American fighter plane squadrons created under the Tuskegee training programme. The pilots were segregated and faced prejudice at the hands of their commanding officers, spending most of their active service grounded and far from any combat. The film had a long and troubled journey to the screen, and Theo had almost forgotten he'd even been part of the film. So much so that it was during an interview at San Diego Comic-Con 2011, while he was promoting another project, he learned *Red Tails* would finally be released in American cinemas in early 2012 – nearly three years after filming had wrapped. In the end, Theo wasn't even mentioned in the film's end credits. The aspiring star was getting his first taste of the frustrations involved in making films and an early lesson in the fickle nature of the industry he was now a part of.

Chapter Three

SHAILENE: THE SECRET LIFE OF AN AMERICAN ACTRESS

SHAILENE'S BIG BREAK CAME IN EARLY 2008, a few months after she had turned sixteen, when she was cast as Amy Juergens in the television series *The Secret Life of the American Teenager*.

The show was to be made by ABC Family, a basic cable channel owned by the Disney Corporation. The channel had a long history in producing kids' cartoons, family oriented television series and made-for-TV movies. In 2006, after years of stagnation and falling viewing figures, ABC Family was overhauled and re-launched, promising a much more sophisticated and mature selection of programmes. Under the tag line 'A New Kind of Family', it had dropped all its pre-school and children's programmes, farming them out to its sister channels Toon Disney and Disney Channel, and aimed to cater more directly to its target audience of teenage girls and young women.

The channel's first original series to showcase these principles was *Kyle XY*. The show, about a mysterious teenage boy who is adopted by an ordinary family in order to help him re-learn the basic human emotions of anger, joy and love proved to be a big hit. The winning formula – a cute lead actor, Matt Dallas, teen drama, romance and sci-fi – gave the newly invigorated channel its first real breakout success.

With renewed confidence, and aiming to hold on to the female viewers who were gravitating towards more adult themed series such as *The Hills*, *Brothers and Sisters*, *Friday Night Lights* and *Ugly Betty* – all of which launched on competing channels that year – ABC Family commissioned *The Secret Life of the American Teenager*. The success of *Gossip Girl*, on rival family channel The CW, highlighted the demand for a show that dealt with real teenage issues, but the increasingly implausible antics of these privileged, wealthy New Yorkers said nothing to most young Americans about what they were experiencing in their own lives. No one on television was talking to them about the real problems they were having growing up – dealing with school, boys and the pressures of everyday teenage life. What they really wanted was to see themselves on screen.

The show was conceived and written by Brenda Hampton, a veteran television producer who had enjoyed success as a writer on *Blossom*, another groundbreaking, issue-led comedy drama, in the early 1990s. Later, she created the similarly clean-cut family saga, *7th Heaven*. Hampton's main goal had always been to create series that the whole family could sit down to and watch together. She told *Entertainment Weekly*: 'I see all my shows as family shows.'

The aim here was to create a series that challenged America's views of teen pregnancy and adolescent relationships in general, while avoiding the obvious clichés about average American teenagers and their lives.

The central character, Amy Juergens, is an ordinary fifteen-year-old girl whom Shailene described to 411Mania.com as 'an extrovert. She's very happy with her life, and she dreams [of going] to Juilliard, and after one night at band camp, she gets pregnant and her whole world comes crashing down.'

The show's first season follows Amy as she discovers, and then initially tries to conceal, her pregnancy, and ends with the final revelation to her parents, the child's father, Ricky, and her supportive new boyfriend, Ben. Shailene told *Girls' Life*, '[Amy] is so complex, she does normal things like school, [deals with] best friend issues, having a first boyfriend and a first love, yet she's also pregnant. That adds a whole other twist to a normal teenager's life.'

Aside from the more trivial problems the average teenager might face, the series aimed to explore, and discuss frankly, subjects such as underage sex, teenage pregnancy, abortion, STDs, the complicated first experiences of relationships and the struggles many young people have to fit in during a period of huge change. Shailene explained to 411Mania.com, 'The show is very unique and very different to any teen show that's ever been on television.' She was struck by the bold and unusual way it dealt with such difficult subjects, continuing, 'This is a teenage show, and it does talk about sex and sexual activities and stuff, but it doesn't make any references to drugs or alcohol, which is very unique in this industry.' She concluded, 'I think [it] puts a positive outlook on teenagers.'

Towards the end of 2007, the casting call went out to the usual long list of agents and casting agencies. ABC Family were looking for a group of young male and female actors who not only had the acting skills and maturity to bring their cast of troubled teen characters to life, but also had the required down-to-earth qualities to make them believable as average American teenagers.

Shailene told SheReality.com that the job that would change her life came her way in a rather mundane fashion. 'It was pretty much like any other audition process. I went in and met with the casting director, and then there was interest there.' She elaborated, 'The series creator [Brenda Hampton] was in the room and she took a liking to me, and then I went to testing. So it was kind of a quick, crazy process that flew by. It all happened so quickly.'

Hampton vividly remembered the audition and told EW.com, 'Before [Shailene] ever walked into the room to audition, I looked at her [photograph] . . . and I said, "She looks like a star." And after reading . . . when Shailene left the room, I said, "She *is* a star."'

The process of casting continued into early 2008. In the first season of the show, Shailene's character, Amy, would have not one, but two, boys fighting for her attention. The part of Ricky Underwood, the father of her baby, would go to Daren Kagasoff, while Kenny Baumann snagged the role of Ben Boykewich, the boy who Amy starts a relationship with after she finds out she is pregnant.

In April 2008, the *Hollywood Reporter* revealed the show's secret weapon would be the casting of Molly Ringwald, who had been hired to play Anne Juergens, Amy's mother. Ringwald, like Shailene, had found fame at an early age. She had become the ultimate teen star of the 1980s through her work with John Hughes in films such as *Sixteen Candles*, *Pretty in Pink* and most successfully *The Breakfast Club*. Alongside actors such as Emilio Estevez, Rob Lowe and Demi Moore she was considered a core member of the infamous 'Brat Pack'. ABC Family president Paul Lee explained to *Entertainment Weekly*, '[She] was critical. She triggered a huge nostalgia audience.'

Ringwald understood the material as she had portrayed her fair share of rebellious teens and good girls falling into temptation. Talking to *Entertainment Weekly*, she said, 'I wasn't sure I was ready to play the mother of a teenager. I felt like I skipped a few steps.' But thankfully she was persuaded to join the cast and the last piece of the *Secret Life* jigsaw was in place.

Shailene revealed her excitement after their first meeting to 411Mania.com: 'She's so down to earth . . . and she smiles all the time. Honestly, she's amazing at what she does.' Shailene's relationship with Ringwald would become a constant source of inspiration and she went on to say, 'She is a great actress, and just by watching her, I can learn from her . . . We just had this connection, which I think is amazing . . . we just feed off of each other.' The pair quickly created a chemistry both on- and off-screen and their genuine relationship formed a stable foundation for much of the show's credibility. It was obvious the whole experience was going to be a hugely enjoyable learning curve for Shailene and she would be a willing sponge, soaking it all up.

After years of playing younger characters due to her youthful appearance, Shailene was finally getting the chance to play a girl of her own age. This was a welcome change and allowed her to show she fully understood the everyday pitfalls of the average American teenager's high school experience. She told 411Mania. com, 'there's the conflict and the pressure of doing things that you don't wanna do.' Expanding on this in an interview with SheReality. com, she said, 'A lot of the characters are going through that stage in high school where you're starting to become a person . . . that recognition of who you are [and] there's a lot of confusion . . . you get scared.'

In the scripts, Amy was shy and introverted; she was an

observer who liked to sit back and watch everything that went on among her friends, but she was also a bit of a snob, could be fairly opinionated and wasn't afraid to give advice – whether her friends wanted it or not. Although she could relate to her character on a basic level, and she obviously understood the politics of the average American high school, it became clear Shailene was going to have to do a lot of research to perfect some of Amy's more negative qualities, as she told *Malibu* magazine: 'Amy complains about everything in her life.' This was definitely not something that could be said about Shailene.

To prepare fully for the role of Amy, Shailene also had to have a deeper understanding of what young pregnant girls like her character went through on a daily basis. What was it really like having a baby while still in high school and coping with the constant pressure of looking after a child, not to mention dealing with other people's prejudice towards young, unmarried mothers? She told 411Mania.com, 'I've seen kids my age get pregnant, and to me it was always like, "How can you be so stupid?" But, then again, sometimes it's not their fault.'

She explained her research had been limited to talking to adults she knew, as she had found it difficult to actually meet girls her own age who were willing to talk to her about their experiences. She said, 'My aunt was pregnant a while ago. [I asked her] "What does it feel like? Is it hard with the morning sickness?" so I can get a sense of what she's going through behind the scenes.'

To prepare her for working with the two babies that would play her son in the show, Shailene would spend an hour playing with the boys before filming started. This proved invaluable. Not only did it give Shailene a much better understanding of the relentless stress involved in being solely responsible for a baby and the loneliness and isolation that many young parents experience, it made her much more confident being alone with a baby and went a long way to making the bond they shared on screen more real.

With the key cast members assembled, shooting began on the Warner Brother's Ranch lot in Los Angeles in early 2008.

The filming schedule for season one was fairly intense and far from flexible, but this is what the whole Woodley family had been in training for all those years. The 'well-oiled machine' came into its own. Years of seamlessly incorporating auditions and acting jobs into Shailene's everyday life meant they were more than capable of coping with the increasing demands and pressures her first long-term, full-time job were throwing at them. They rode the storm, making sure Shailene's timetable was managed and organized in a way that allowed her to continue attending her normal classes at Simi Valley High School and, therefore, did not disrupt her education or affect her all-important friendships.

In comparison with most television shows, *Secret Life* had a fairly large cast of younger actors. This meant that there was often a very lively and informal atmosphere on set. Shailene recalled the early days in an interview with SheReality.com. 'When the show first started we all kind of just got put there together. It's not like any of us got to choose who we got to work with or who we were going to spend the [next] two years of our lives, and hopefully more, with.' She went on to describe the growing solidarity between the cast: 'Everyone bonded immediately; it was kind of that thing where we didn't really have a choice, so we bonded, and it's been great.'

Although she'd spent a lot of time working as a guest on single episodes of established television shows, for the first time in her life she was spending more time with a group of like-minded, focused young actors, having fun and forging strong relationships. 'A lot of us are very different people, but there [are] never conflicts; sometimes there's a difference in opinions, but we're all so down to earth about it and we all just accept each other as who we are and we learn from each other.'

The members of the predominately young cast fed off each other's different personal experiences and enthusiasms. They would sit around for hours watching YouTube videos, sharing their musical preferences – some liked hip-hop and others liked indie or rock – but they would listen patiently to each other's favourite bands and learn from their varied tastes. She would tell the TV Chick website, 'I just really love working with all the cast. It's so much fun when everyone's on set. When we have eighteen people on set at once and we're all jamming in the trailers – on guitars or singing.' She confessed with a smile, 'The girls – we are huge Willow Smith fans – so we'll put on "Whip My Hair" and we'll whip our hair for hours. It's pretty fun.'

Talking to *Girls' Life* magazine, she also recalled the times the cast spent playing Britney Spears videos, singing along, pretending to be her. 'Everybody gets all crazy – it's pretty funny when the guys do it!'

Her relationships with Ken Baumann and Daren Kagasoff, the actors playing Ben and Ricky respectively, mirrored their on-screen chemistry. 'It's really fun to work with both of them. The scenes [we have together] are very different because Amy is more flirtatious with Ricky than Ben. Daren and I like to go back and forth about [that] and then Kenny and I are more serious about it.'

These friendships began to spill over into her time away from the show, she told 411Mania.com. 'On weekends, we'll hang out, and we'll go to dinner sometimes. We just mesh together, and we've created such strong relationships so quickly that it's kind of like a brother–sister scenario.' Shailene formed an especially strong bond with Megan Park, who played Grace Bowman on the show. The pair became fast friends during the long hours waiting around on set between takes. It was Megan who began teaching Shailene how to play guitar.

Brenda Hampton, the show's creative force, emphasized to EW.com the friendly family atmosphere she had always tried to maintain on the *Secret Life* set. 'I strive to create an environment where everyone can enjoy the work and do their best.' She was quick to point out what they had achieved was fairly unique: '[usually] that's an impossible goal. I can get a show done on time and under budget . . . but making a production a good experience where everyone still has time for a life . . . that's a rare experience in Hollywood.'

Shailene was experiencing something new. Her passion for acting was beginning to grow, feeding off the energy and collaborative environment on the *Secret Life* set, and a whole new world of possibility had started to open up.

Shailene summed up what she was going through to 411Mania. com in the weeks before the show was aired. 'When you go on a TV show as a guest star, you don't have time to really analyse your character. On this show, you get to set every single day, and every day that you go, your character becomes deeper and deeper, and you get more wrapped around who she actually is.' She further detailed the ease with which she was finding the transformation from being herself to becoming Amy on set: 'It's such a great experience to be able to know your character so well that you can just dive into it the second they say "action."' She was adapting well to the working methods and the artistic advantages of having a regular television gig. She told Movie Online, 'You do get to know the characters so well and you know every single thing about them, so when you're memorizing lines it takes you two seconds because you know exactly how your character is going to say them and you know exactly how the other characters are going to respond. It is beautiful to watch these characters grow up.'

The Secret Life of the American Teenager debuted on ABC Family on 1 July 2008. The ABC Family marketing department went into overdrive as the show was launched with a huge publicity burst. The subject matter may have been slightly controversial and potentially tricky to promote to some sections of the general public, but it was an easy sell to the press and was obviously going to polarize any media reaction.

A review in the *Pittsburgh Post-Gazette* was a fairly typical example of *Secret Life*'s wider reception, preferring to give the programme the benefit of the doubt. The paper stated that 'it is by no means a conventionally edgy show', and went on to praise the depiction of some of its more clichéd character types as real people rather than as 'the butt of jokes', finishing with a fairly positive conclusion: 'it's far more realistic in scope and situation than *Gossip Girl*.'

Unfortunately, not everyone in the press had fallen in love with the show's mix of teen drama and controversial social issues. Widely reviewed, and the subject of countless articles, *Secret Life*, while not being a critical disaster, failed to win over the majority of mainstream critics. Ken Tucker of *Entertainment Weekly* said the show was 'filled with [moral] messages and a lotta wooden acting', while *The New York Times* slated the show for its heavy-handedness and claimed the filmmakers had an anti-pregnancy agenda, writing, 'ABC Family means well but could not have done worse. *Secret Life* doesn't take the fun out of teenage pregnancy, it takes the fun out of television.' *Variety* magazine was quick to dismiss the show, saying, '[It] wants to be a slow-motion version of *Juno* but settles for being an obvious, stereotype-laden teen soap.' The magazine concluded, 'based on first impressions, *The Secret Life . . .* should probably stay a secret.'

However, the people reviewing *Secret Life* were not the ones who had been crying out for this kind of series, and they were definitely not the audience the show had been created to satisfy. The day after the first episode aired, EW.com asked its readers, 'How well did *Secret Life* represent the American teen? Did anything make you blush and go "yeah, me too", or were you stuck rolling your eyes and wishing for more Ringwald?' The answer was clearly the former as the show scored a clear bull's-eye with ABC Family's target market of teenage girls and young women, and it was they who tuned in – in their millions – to the show's first episode. Creator and writer Brenda Hampton said at the time, 'I'd rather get good ratings and bad reviews than bad ratings and good reviews.' She definitely got her wish. *The Secret Life of the American Teenager* delivered the channel's highest ratings for the first episode of an original scripted show in its history. And, although the mainstream press reaction was largely negative, one person was receiving universal praise: Shailene.

The New York *Daily News* review was a characteristic example, proclaiming, 'Shailene Woodley is terrific as [Amy]', while going on to sum up the widely held consensus that, 'for [*Secret Life*] to work, Woodley probably needs to carry both the baby and the show.' *Entertainment Weekly*'s Ken Tucker said, 'Woodley is utterly beguiling: an anti-*Gossip Girl*.' He went on to say, 'Like a great silent film actress, she has a face that conveys shades of anguish and joy. Her performance lifts a well-meaning, rather brave, but ramshackle show a notch. And it needs all the notch-raising it can get.'

By the time the show ended its initial run of eleven episodes on 9 September 2008, ABC Family realized they had a genuine ratings hit on their hands. It's no surprise that, after such an incredible start, they were keen to exploit the success of *Secret Life*. Before the show had returned to air the second half of its first season – a further twelve episodes – on 5 January 2009, it was announced that a second series had been commissioned and production was due to start in early spring. ABC Family president, Paul Lee, explained the impact the show had on turning his channel – having unanimously been perceived and dismissed as a minority youth channel – into a major player. '*Secret Life* put us culturally on the map. On cable, it takes a *Sopranos* or a *Shield* or a *Secret Life* to really crystalize a network for the audience.'

Secret Life's average audience of 4 million viewers was eclipsing the viewing figures of the similarly newsworthy *Gossip Girl* by well over a million. *The Secret Life of the American Teenager* had instantly become the channel's flagship show and, as such, every effort would be made to ensure this ship stayed afloat.

The initial success of the series was a much more personal victory for Shailene. She had wanted to bring something real to the character of Amy, a likeability that wasn't necessarily in the original script. She had also wanted the chance to educate the audience and challenge any preconceptions about the subject matter. She told *Entertainment Weekly*, 'I feel like the themes are realistic, but the way they present them are definitely artistically licensed. We definitely showed it was not glamorous.' She expanded upon this in an interview with 411Mania.com at the time, saying, 'I feel so fortunate to be able to have this opportunity, as an actress, to be able to take the time to actually form who Amy Juergens is.' It's lucky she felt that way, because, for Shailene, this was the beginning of what eventually became a five-year relationship with Amy and *The Secret Life of the American Teenager*.

And, as the storylines undoubtedly became increasingly far-fetched and 'soapy', the heart of the show remained the issues involved in maintaining real relationships – be it romantic, amicable or familial – and the problems that affected most average American teenagers every day. Over the course of the five seasons, viewers would see Amy develop into a much more rounded character, undoubtedly absorbing and reflecting a great deal of Shailene's own independent spirit and growing confidence.

The series finale saw Amy finally accept that she needed to follow her dream and, with much deliberation, she made the brave decision to head to New York to study at university alone, leaving her son behind with his father. The very last scene showed Ricky reading John a bedtime story with the line, 'And she lived happily ever after, and so will we.'

The fans' response to Shailene and her character Amy was nothing short of incredible. Her key role to the show's story and themes meant she became the unofficial spokesperson for the series. A heavy burden for someone who was just about to turn seventeen but, typically, Shailene approached it with maturity and a determination to keep a spotlight on the real issues *Secret Life* highlighted.

In an interview with EW.com, Shailene was keen to point out that during the course of filming, and through her own research, she had been forced to reconsider some of her earlier, uninformed, views on teenage pregnancy, and had found real empathy for girls her age who found themselves in the same predicament as Amy. 'It's really sad what those girls are going through. It's weird to think that they're going through what I pretend to go through. It's trippy to think that people really deal with this stuff.'

Talking to the *Huffington Post*, Shailene discussed the constructive feedback she'd had from parents who had watched *Secret Life* with their own sons and daughters. 'The most positive compliment I've ever gotten was from a mother who came up to me and said, "Thank you [to you] and your writers, because it has opened up conversation outlets within our home … I can talk about sex now, and I can talk about the consequences of it … I would have never talked about that with my teenagers."' Shailene concluded, 'that's where I think a lot of people get lost in teenage sexuality, because they're uneducated in it.' She told SheReality.com, 'I think it's really incredible [to be] able to talk about how certain things happen and why they happen and kind of go through all that and be comfortable around their children.'

Responding to the many who had praised the show's frank attitude towards sensitive issues and the avenues of discussion it provided, Shailene admitted, 'That's really inspiring to me to just know that we opened up communication in households that might not necessarily [have] talked about it before.' It would be the first of many campaigns Shailene would pursue to combat poor education on certain topics.

Praise came in a different form as she received several award nominations for her first year on *Secret Life*. She scored nods at the Teen Choice Awards, where *Secret Life* won the award for Choice Summer TV Show, and at the Young Artist Awards for best performance by a leading actress, where she was in esteemed company alongside Miley Cyrus, Selena Gomez, Miranda Cosgrove and Taylor Momsen. She finally won her first acting prize when she picked up the award for Outstanding Female Rising Star in a Drama Series at the Gracie Allen Awards in 2010. Flushed with success, she told 411Mania.com, '[It's] the first time I'm getting attention for my work, and it's definitely strange and definitely not what I'm used to.' Ever keen to stress she still wasn't taking it all too seriously, she continued, 'I think it's all about figuring out who you are and knowing that everyone is the same.'

The Woodley family's strategy to keep Shailene's feet on the ground and their strenuous efforts to maintain her normal home life had paid off. Shailene thought the real reward at the end of her first year in the *Secret Life* spotlight was holding onto her down-to-earth outlook on life. 'Just because you might be on TV does not make you better than another person. And, for me, I feel like I haven't gotten caught up in Hollywood.' When asked what she treasured most, she stated, 'I don't have very many friends who are actually in the industry, so I guess just coming home and living my normal life with my friends – my best friends – [and] my mom's cooking.' Unfortunately, that peaceful equilibrium was about to be shattered.

As *The Secret Life of the American Teenager* moved into its second year, Shailene's role as Amy was as central to the show as it had been in the first season. The shooting schedule, now including interviews and promotional work, had got out of control. No amount of precision planning and teamwork on the behalf of the Woodley's could make the increased working days – sometimes eight to fourteen hours – fit with Shailene's regular school hours.

With a heavy heart, Shailene decided she needed to stop

attending her normal classes, leave behind her high school and her best friends and start work with a private tutor. Her principal allowed her to remain registered as a student at the school, so that eventually she would be allowed to graduate alongside her classmates.

So began a hectic period of long days on set, doing homework whenever and wherever possible between takes in her trailer. Then once a week, a teacher from her old school would come to her house to run through all the work she had missed. She continued with this chaotic timetable for the next year, until she finished high school. She told *Girls' Life*, 'I didn't get to be with my friends all the time, and I missed being in class and messing around with them.' But she was eager to stress that she realized how lucky she was. 'The show is the most amazing thing that's ever happened to me, but there was a price I had to pay.'

As one of the standout performers involved in *Secret Life*, and a key element in the show's success, Shailene was attracting a lot of attention. But she would begin to experience the full extent of 'the price' she had to pay, and the undoubted frustrations that went with it.

The standard contract for most US television shows – usually signed before a single episode has even been filmed – ties the main cast to the show for a minimum of seven years. ABC Family's standard contract was for six. While protecting the programme makers from lengthy – and possibly messy – negotiations at the start of every year a show is renewed, this arrangement can prove problematic for the actors. If a show is successful, it may be a double-edged sword: working on a high-profile show could bring in a lot of attention and offers to participate in other projects, but the standard work pattern for a twenty-four episode television season is a three months on, three months off rolling schedule, restricting time in between seasons to undertake these other acting jobs. This is acceptable to actors who enjoy working on the show; however, if the actor is unsettled and wants to leave, it can prove very difficult to get out of the contract. Aside from the financial losses this can incur, it can damage a reputation as a reliable and trustworthy actor. Shailene remained positive about such a lack of flexibility in her schedule, telling Moviefone.com, 'I've learned a lot about making commitments and really paying attention to the material that you work on.'

Despite her busy shooting timetable, Shailene was able to attend her high school prom with her old school friends and she graduated – with mostly A grades – alongside the rest of her Simi Valley High School class of 2009. At this point, true to her 'acting is just a hobby' philosophy, Shailene was squeezing in some extra advanced courses in preparation for applying to colleges. She told *Girls' Life*, 'I've always wanted to go to NYU (New York University), so that's definitely a possibility', but within a few months of finding out the show had been picked up for a second year, her contract effectively tying her to *Secret Life* for the foreseeable future, Shailene realized studying in New York was an unrealistic pipe dream. Her ultimate goals were still fairly unclear, but she spoke of studying interior design, exploring her already flourishing interest in environmental issues, natural healing, or even following in her parents' footsteps, both of whom have psychology degrees.

The truth was that her calendar was pretty full for the next few years and offers of work outside the confines of *Secret Life* were now filtering through. Even when Shailene was on a scheduled break or on season hiatus from the show, her specific contract meant she was still officially working for, and thus representing,

ABC Family. This meant the family-orientated channel would take a first look at any other acting jobs she was offered. It removed from Shailene the freedom of choice in her own career and gave the *Secret Life* producers the power to rule out certain auditions if they didn't think the subject matter of the project fitted with the image of the network, Shailene's character on the show, or if the timings didn't synchronize with her increasingly busy schedule. Unable to take time off to attend every audition she would have liked to, Shailene saw parts in movies and other television shows get offered to her contemporaries and she became frustrated that she was missing out on important opportunities to advance her career and test herself as an actress.

She explained the situation to the *Los Angeles Times*: 'It's difficult when you have a show. Even though [the network] is great and they let me out, if it's not the right movie, they tend to not let you [do it].' Shailene wanted to make sure people knew she wasn't afraid to work hard or stick with the commitment she'd made to *Secret Life*. She realized the show's producers may be throwing up short-term obstacles, but it would definitely be worth it in terms of achieving her long-term goal – acting on the big screen.

She has stated that there are several 'auteur' directors she'd like to work with – including Danny Boyle, Darren Aronofsky and Terrence Malick. But, as if to prove her lack of movie buff credentials, in an interview with *Time Out Chicago*, when quizzed about her favourite Malick movie she said, 'Maybe if you name some, I'll remember which ones I've seen.' She still had a little to learn about massaging the egos of the Hollywood elite!

Shailene also name-checked other actresses who found fame at an early age, such as Natalie Portman and Reese Witherspoon, as her inspiration. She singled out Dakota Fanning as a particular role model in an interview with *Girls' Life*. '[Dakota] is just phenomenal. Look at how much she's accomplished so far in her life – it's incredible . . . Obviously [like her], I want to do a lot of movies.'

Shailene was ever the optimist and keen to further demonstrate her 'everything happens for a reason' philosophy. She told the *Hollywood Reporter*, 'It's been this ladder that I've been climbing and I'm still climbing.'

Her diplomacy, in what must have been a frustrating situation, is to be admired. It may also have proved to be a very sensible response. Not rocking the boat too much at ABC Family and biding her time was about to pay off – in a big way.

Chapter Four

THEO: MAD ABOUT THE BOY

After leaving the Bristol Old Vic Theatre School in 2009, Theo's next job was in a BBC drama entitled *A Passionate Woman*, written by Kay Mellor.

Mellor is a well-established script writer who has worked in television since the mid-1980s. She started as a writer on *Coronation Street* and contributed to Channel 4's *Brookside* before creating soap opera *Families* for Granada Television. She then wrote several extremely popular comedy drama series including *Band of Gold*, *Playing the Field* and *Fat Friends*. *A Passionate Woman*, written as a play and originally staged at West Yorkshire Playhouse in 1992, was based on the true story of Mellor's own mother's experiences. As a stage show it had gone on to be a huge hit with several different productions around the world.

The television adaptation centred on the life and loves of an ordinary working-class woman, whose story is told in two sections; the first, taking place in 1958, and the second, picking up almost thirty years later, in 1985.

In 1958, Betty – played by Billie Piper – is a newly married young mother who begins an unexpected and passionate affair with her married Polish neighbour, Theo's character, Craze. The affair is brief, but has far-reaching effects for Betty and her family. Craze is murdered by his wife when she finds out about the affair and Betty has to bury the truth, keeping the affair a secret to try to forget the man she thinks is the love of her life. Betty lives with her deception until 1985 when, as she prepares for her only son's wedding, all her long-concealed passions are revealed.

Theo is well cast as Craze, the charming Polish man who sweeps Betty off her feet and turns her into the passionate woman of the title. There is no doubt that Theo's Mediterranean good looks were a key factor in seeing him cast as the exotic and charismatic stranger, yet he brings so much more to the role. While the character of Craze is eventually revealed to be a rogue and a womanizer, in the beginning he has to be convincingly likeable and charming. There is no getting away from the devilish twinkle in Theo's eyes, or his natural seductive magnetism, but he also brings a softness and boyish appeal to the character. Theo and his co-star, former *Doctor Who* companion Billie Piper, worked well together, maintaining a powerful on-screen chemistry. Piper spoke on the DVD extras about the intensity of the production, the long hours on set and how the limited budget meant each day's filming was precious, with no room for delays or mistakes. She had nothing but praise for Theo, stating he helped keep the energy and atmosphere on set positive with his infectious humour, pranks and high spirits.

It was becoming obvious that, despite his theatre training, Theo was a natural screen actor. The camera loved him and he was developing a real understanding of what was needed to survive the demands of working on a busy set and the stresses of a hectic filming schedule.

Theo's next job was to be one of his briefest, but crucially, it was to have a considerable impact on his career.

Downton Abbey was conceived as an Edwardian-era drama set in a fictional Yorkshire country estate and would see the return of the historic 'family saga', a genre of television that had seen its heyday with the likes of *The Forsyte Saga* and *Upstairs, Downstairs* in the late 1960s and early 1970s. This type of drama had all but disappeared from British television screens, considered old-fashioned and out of step with what modern audiences wanted. Period dramas of this kind are extremely expensive to make, and so *Downton Abbey* would be a co-production between ITV and the American PBS network. It was this American connection that was to prove essential to the unprecedented success of the show.

Former actor turned writer, Julian Fellowes, was commissioned to write the series due to his familiarity with the subject matter. Fellowes had achieved success as a screenwriter when his script for *Gosford Park* won the Oscar for Best Original Screenplay in 2002. The film, directed by Robert Altman, was an old-fashioned murder mystery set in a stately home, centred round the complicated lives and loves of both the 'upstairs' aristocrats and the 'downstairs' servants. He would go on to write several high-profile projects, including a stage musical adaptation of *Mary Poppins* and film scripts featuring Hollywood A-listers Johnny Depp and Angelina Jolie (*The Tourist*), Emily Blunt (*Young Victoria*) and Reese Witherspoon (*Vanity Fair*). But his biggest success would see him return to the familiar territory he had so successfully explored in *Gosford Park*.

The producers of *Downton Abbey* were looking for a young

actor to play an enchanting, foreign visitor and they were suitably impressed with the exotic glamour of Theo's Greek ancestry, which he'd used to such great effect in *A Passionate Woman* – it seemed Theo was carving a lucrative niche for himself as the mysterious foreign charmer. He was cast as Kemal Pamuk, a Turkish diplomat who, while visiting Downton, takes a shine to Lord and Lady Grantham's eldest daughter, Mary. Theo's masculinity and confidence were a perfect fit for the cocksure but engaging Mr Pamuk. Lord Grantham himself describes him as 'quite a treat for the ladies'.

Theo would get the chance to show off his horse-riding skills and no-one looked better in the smart riding attire than him – even if he was wearing a rather unflattering dishevelled wig. Soon the whole of *Downton*'s female population is swooning under the spell of his irresistible allure. His clipped English accent perfectly suggests a wealthy foreign student, fresh from his education at one of the finest schools in England. Theo's performance is tinged with humour as Pamuk lustily tries to woo Lady Mary. Although the attraction is mutual, Mary knows her reputation, as well as that of her family, could not allow anything more to happen. Luckily, Mr Pamuk's charms are also working on Thomas the footman, who readily admits, 'I'm very attracted to Turkish culture'. Pamuk uses the threat of exposing Thomas's advances to blackmail him into escorting him to Lady Mary's bedroom later that evening. Again, Theo's playful acting style injects the seduction scene with a roguish lasciviousness and just enough humour for it not to be too crude or too comical.

Unfortunately for Mr Pamuk – and Theo – the exertions in Lady Mary's bed end in a lethal heart attack and Theo plays out the rest of the episode as a corpse. Although his time on *Downton* was brief, it would have a far-reaching impact on his career and the after-effects of the Pamuk storyline were still being felt as the show entered its fourth series in late 2013.

Downton Abbey was shown in America on PBS and quickly became a ratings phenomenon. Along the way it picked up a diverse array of famous admirers, with Katy Perry, Simon Pegg, Josh Groban, Joan Rivers, Jonathan Ross and Mindy Kaling all expressing their love for the show, while some huge Hollywood stars, including Tom Hanks, Sarah Jessica Parker and Harrison Ford have also spoken about how much they enjoy *Downton*. The ultimate seal of approval came when Prince William and Kate Middleton told a reporter at the *Telegraph* that they were 'huge fans of the show'. Eventually, Theo began to get 'shout-outs' from *Downton* fans in America, he told *Cosmopolitan*. 'Obviously, it's awesome to be recognized and the show is a great piece of work, but I suppose it is strange because [I am] only in about twenty minutes of one episode . . . the ratio of work I actually did to all the talk about it . . . it feels a bit fraudulent.' He added with a laugh, 'They should have paid me more!' He even admitted that, apart from the episode he was in, he hadn't watched any more *Downton*. He went on to tell *The New York Times* he was reluctant to take any credit for the show's success or try and use its popularity to his advantage, saying he didn't like 'reflecting on it too much because I was only in one episode'.

He may not have wanted to talk about it, but it had proved to be an invaluable experience. Being attached to such a successful show was never going to hurt and he'd shown he was becoming a much more versatile actor. There was no denying his looks were a huge advantage in some areas as his career progressed, but his acting skills were growing and he had developed a lightness of touch that made him perfect as a believable and likeable leading man.

Shortly after the *Downton Abbey* episode aired, Theo was cast as Jed Harper, the male lead in another UK-produced television series, *Bedlam*.

Creators David Allison, Neil Jones and Chris Parker were looking to create something that had the same mix of supernatural and sexy that had turned US shows like *True Blood*, *The Vampire Diaries* and *Supernatural* into hugely popular international franchises. They were keen to tap into the UK's long and rich history of producing inventive and thought-provoking science fiction series such as *Blake's 7*, *The Tomorrow People* and *Sapphire and Steel*. But it was the unprecedented success of the rebooted *Doctor Who* and emerging genre series such as *Merlin*, *Being Human* and *Primeval* that kick-started the renaissance. UK television audiences were now experiencing a new era of UK-produced science fiction and fantasy.

Allison, Jones and Parker locked themselves away in a hotel conference room for a weekend and threw around as many ideas as they could. *Bedlam* was conceived as a simple twist on the traditional haunted house genre and, as such, offered a variety of possibilities to tell interesting and, hopefully, scary stories. Such a simple pitch really stood out, so much so that this original idea remained more or less unaltered from its genesis, through production and into the finished show.

Set in a former mental asylum that had been renovated into a block of upmarket apartments known as Bedlam Heights, the show uncovered the building's infamous past, its many hidden secrets and the spooky hauntings that occur there. Allison told Uinterview.com, 'We were very clear it had to have a "ghost of the week". But, for us, the serial story was at least as important.' Their aim was to create a long-running series, and they planned to keep viewers hooked with an ongoing, slowly revealed mystery involving the main characters.

The blueprint for the show was the UK series *Tales of the Unexpected*, which ran from 1979 to 1988. Allison explained to Uinterview.com, 'It wasn't horror. It was just freaky tales. I think that really influenced us, weirdly, because it was all about the story. We wanted to have that kind of sense, that it was scary on the page. We don't want to rely on special effects.' The visual style was to involve mostly practical special effects, relying on creepy lighting, creative sound design and the power of suggestion rather than expensive CGI. Allison stated he wanted the show to have the same no-nonsense sensibility as its American cousin *Supernatural.* 'We wanted a very clear pre-title sequence, high octane. We also wanted it to look dark and creepy, but kind of sexy as well.'

Alongside the elements of traditional British gothic horror and the more contemporary fast-paced storytelling there would be the influence of Japanese horror films such as *The Ring* and *Dark Water.* Allison stated '[these films are] all about the fear of what you might see, and I think the best type of supernatural storytelling is about the fear'. He concluded, '*Bedlam* is really just [about] what's inside the box.'

This vibrant style and pacing would be key to attracting the younger audience they needed to make the show a hit, but the thing that would get social media buzzing and eyes glued to screens would be a cast of sexy, good-looking twenty-something actors.

Theo was cast to play Jed, a troubled young man who returns to Bedlam Heights in mysterious circumstances. He was joined by Charlotte Salt, who played Kate Bettany, Jed's adopted cousin and the co-owner and manager of Bedlam Heights with her father, Warren. Molly and Ryan, Kate's best friends and flatmates, would be played by Ashley Madekwe and *Pop Idol* winner Will Young respectively.

Theo's character is central to virtually everything that happens in the show, as early in the first episode Jed is revealed to have the ability to see and communicate with ghosts. Theo loved the basic concept of the show and was keen to explore the darker, supernatural elements of the series, telling the Assignment X website, 'Human nature is scary in terms of what it can do, [but] a ghost is something you can't explain; something you can't control can be pretty dangerous.' Jed had ended up a loner and a drifter, dealing with the consequences of his decision to isolate himself from his friends and family in order to try to understand his 'illness'. As the story unfolds we learn he has had this ability his whole life and spent most of his childhood institutionalized to the point he ended up estranged from Kate and the rest of his adopted family. Now Jed is an adult, he's taken control and has spent the last few years using his psychic abilities to help spirits 'pass over'. Clearly, Jed is a very complex character, and the validity of the show would rest heavily on Theo's shoulders.

Bedlam creator David Allison told Uinterview.com, 'We didn't want Jed to have a superpower. He has to deal with each ghost . . . maybe sometimes he doesn't succeed. That makes it so much more interesting.'

Theo was definitely up for the challenge and began creating an extensive history for Jed. In an interview with CraveOnline he said, 'I wanted to figure out every single detail of his life from when he began having visions. Was he thrown out of school? What were his first visions? Who was his first doctor? How was he diagnosed with paranoid schizophrenia? What drugs had he been fed?' He further explained the long-term effects his treatment may have had on his character to the Assignment X website. 'He's been plied with drugs and had all this stuff happen to him. I think [that] makes for quite a complex person and so he probably wouldn't be cracking jokes.' He concluded, 'The fact that he sees visions . . . we wanted to make sure they were physically painful, visually arresting and had a real effect on people. So as a result, I think he would be a fairly dark person.'

Armed with Jed's back-story, his next job would be figuring out what the consequences of these supernatural encounters were for Jed. 'We wanted him not to just see ghosts . . . they're more like visions and they physically affect him quite strongly,' he explained to the website. 'It's like an epileptic fit. It's a barrage of information and sensory emotion and anger and violence in his brain . . . his body is convulsing in his reaction to it so he comes out of a vision really depleted and in pain.' He concluded, 'That's why it's such a burden for him.'

Undoubtedly the show was attempting to achieve quite a balancing act: characters who would be relatable enough to drive the human side of the story while making sure the supernatural elements at the heart of the show were exciting and dramatic without overpowering everything else – and a lot of that depended on Theo's central role, which straddled the two main strands of the series. He didn't take that responsibility lightly and was keen to make sure *Bedlam* was not seen as 'just another fantasy show'. He told Variety.com, 'It's still a drama about young people, and you have to grab the realism to make it work.'

Aside from the more creative aspects of the acting process

and conveying the darker elements of Jed's character in a realistic fashion, Theo was very aware that the show's other main objective was to be fun and sexy, and he didn't hold back on that front, either – in the first episode, Theo spends most of his screen time shirtless, wearing only a towel or naked in the bathtub.

The majority of filming took place in Manchester, with Bangor University standing in for the exterior of Bedlam Heights. Filming away from home for nearly three months, the cast bonded quickly and became a close-knit group, with Theo forming an especially strong bond with Will Young. It's safe to assume that Theo's interest in music and his time spent singing in bands was a major factor in cementing their friendship. Young was using the *Bedlam* job as the opportunity to take a break from finishing his latest album, *Echoes*, and he and Theo spent a lot of time together on and off set. With an obvious reference to Theo, Will jokingly told one interviewer that his ego had taken quite a beating having to work with cast members who were 'younger and better actors' than him. The whole cast would spend their evenings together and were able to hit the Manchester scene in relative anonymity, although, on one occasion, Theo recalled pretending to be Will Young's security for an entire evening!

As with any television show, the actors spent a lot of time on set waiting around for scenes to be put up. This process is especially time consuming when it involves lots of unpredictable special effects. Theo recollected the frustration of working this way to the Assignment X website. 'Sometimes you have to really work hard to keep yourself in the zone, especially when you're waiting for forty minutes or longer, [maybe] two hours, between takes . . . or if something's going wrong . . . but that's all part of the job. I think you just have to be mentally really on it all the time.'

That being said, the set was relatively informal and lively, with Theo admitting he spent a lot of time playing practical jokes on his fellow cast members – hiding in cupboards and beat-boxing with Will Young between takes. Young told CultBox, 'Theo made me laugh on set, which is very unfair! We end quite a few of our scenes with dramatic one-liners . . . I couldn't look at his eyes in quite a few scenes and just looked at his shoulder; otherwise he would have made me laugh. We basically lost our professionalism!'

The show began airing on Sky Living in the UK in February 2011. The critical response was fairly mixed and ratings were middling, although they remained steady through the six-episode run. It was Theo who was singled out for praise by *Variety* magazine, who said, '[Theo James] fits the bill as a pretty-boy lead, and benefits from portraying the only character with a compelling hook.'

Although it never became a ratings hit, *Bedlam* had a small, very passionate audience and a dedicated creative team who were keen to fully explore the potential they'd seen in the show's original premise. In the end, a second series was commissioned, but Theo's busy schedule meant he was unable to return to the show and *EastEnders* actress Lacey Turner took over duties as the lead character, Ellie, who is similarly troubled with psychic gifts and is drawn by unknown forces to stay at Bedlam Heights.

Next for Theo was *Room at the Top*. This was a remake of the classic 1959 British film, based on the hugely popular – and hugely shocking, for its time – novel by John Braine. (Coincidentally, a poster for this film can be seen outside the cinema that acts as the meeting place for Craze and Betty in Theo's first major television project, *A Passionate Woman*.) The 2012 version of *Room at the*

Top was made for the BBC as part of BBC4's Original Drama series. It would star Matthew McNulty as Joe Lampton, the ambitious young accountant who plans, by seducing the daughter of his boss, to marry into a wealthy family while also having an affair with an older, married woman, Alice Aisgill, played by Maxine Peake. Much of the shock value of the original telling was lost, over fifty years on from its original publication, but the story of ambition, greed and eventual tragedy was still as relevant and powerful as ever. It stands as an interesting side-note on Theo's CV. He was cast in a relatively small role as one of the other office boys, Jack Wales, who works alongside Joe Lampton at the accountancy firm and appears in only a couple of scenes. An interesting period piece, its leisurely pace and old-fashioned, melodramatic tone are given weight with solid performances from the cast and the beauty and attention to detail in the production.

Originally scheduled to be shown in April 2011, the series was pulled from the BBC listings the day before transmission. A last-minute dispute over who actually owned the film rights threatened to see the project shelved and never broadcast. The series would eventually see the light of day almost a year later when it was shown over two consecutive nights in September 2012.

Theo then took his most unlikable role yet – as James in *The Inbetweeners Movie*. The film was a spin-off from the television series about four geeky teenagers in their A-level years at school. The show had little more than a cult following by the end of its first series, with each episode attracting around 400,000 viewers. However, fuelled by constant repeats and DVD box set binge watching, the show finished its final series as a genuine ratings hit – the finale episode was watched by nearly 4 million. If another series wasn't possible – it was, after all, the story of schoolboys who had now left school, not to mention the fact that most of the actors were now in their mid- to late twenties – a standalone film was the logical next step.

The film would see the boys jetting off to Malia in Crete, taking their first foreign holiday together. Theo was cast as an arrogant holiday rep who is dating the ex-girlfriend of one of the main characters. Theo was likely chosen in this part for his good looks – a necessary feature of the role – but by playing a show-off and a bully, he was cast very much against type. His main scenes involve him intentionally and repeatedly embarrassing one of the boys, Simon, in front of his friends. We first see him, as James, accidentally run Simon over on a quad bike, knocking him to the ground. He is hilariously dismissive, refusing to acknowledge him as he drives off with Simon's ex-girlfriend, Carli. The boys are desperate to raise money to buy tickets for the end of holiday boat party, and we next see Theo in another very funny scene where he persuades Simon to sell him all his clothes (including the ones he's actually wearing) in return for the cash he needs to attend the party. Theo leaves Simon naked on the street, refusing to give him the money he promised him. All Theo's remaining scenes take place at the party on board the boat. Theo's character is being suitably obnoxious, insulting the boys and their prospective girlfriends. He demands that the boys give him a banknote to use to take drugs. They give him a €20 note one of them had earlier concealed in his bottom. Theo's last scene has him unwittingly flirting with girls with a blob of faeces on the end of his nose. The look of confusion on his face as they walk away disgusted is priceless.

The film was shot during the off-season in February 2011 in Magaluf, Mallorca, which stood in for Malia in Crete. The weather during filming was understandably unreliable and the shoot was delayed by rain on several occasions. Despite the weather, the main cast were determined to create the illusion they were enjoying blistering sunshine and everything that goes with it, and ultimately it turned out to be a very enjoyable experience for Theo. Even though he only had a few days on set, he managed to make a very strong impression with his character in the film and he successfully delivered his first truly comic performance.

The film was released in August 2011 and went on to gross nearly £58 million from its £3.5 million budget. At that point, *The Inbetweeners Movie* had been the most successful film Theo had been attached to. That was all about to change with his next project – he was about to star in his first big-budget American film. He was heading to Hollywood – well, Vancouver, Canada, actually – to film *Underworld: Awakening*.

Chapter Five

SHAILENE: A FAMILY AFFAIR

SHAILENE HAD BEEN SENT AN EARLY DRAFT OF A SCRIPT by her agent while she was filming season two of *The Secret Life of the American Teenager*. The draft script, whose vivid characters instantly jumped out at her, was *The Descendants*, the adaptation of Kaui Hart Hemmings's debut novel. The story is loosely based on people Hemmings knew and her own experiences growing up in her native Hawaii. The film rights had been snapped up immediately and the script was still being developed when Shailene received it, but it had not yet found a director.

Shailene told the *Hollywood Reporter* how she 'immediately became so enthralled with it, so passionate about it. I loved how human it was, and how raw it was, and how it didn't cover up any of the messy s*** that goes on in everyday life, 'cause so many Hollywood films do.' She went on to tell Collider.com, 'So many times, you get a script and it says, "and then the character cries", and you read the lines and think, "that would never make me cry." Those lines are so untruthful.'

As someone who had faced the harsh reality of her parents'

divorce and experienced the fall-out from that situation, the true emotions that were expressed in the script and the frankness of its dialogue must have seemed like a welcome relief from the more sanitized family-oriented scripts she was receiving for *Secret Life*. She explained to *BlackBook* magazine, 'Alexander [Payne, the eventual director] wasn't even attached when I first read the script... so the script we ended up using was completely different. However, the story was the same so it fuelled something inside me. I don't remember the last time I was so passionate about something in my life.'

She was especially drawn to the character of Alexandra 'Alex' King, the troubled seventeen-year-old daughter of main character, Matt King. She told the *Ventura County Star*, 'The script affected me, I didn't even need to see the movie to be moved, as I was so moved by the words.' It was shortly after this point that the script finally fell into the hands of auteur filmmaker, Alexander Payne.

Payne had achieved a degree of success and acclaim usually reserved for independent filmmaker veterans such as Woody Allen or the Coen brothers with his first few movies – *Election*, *About Schmidt* and *Sideways*.

Election starred Reese Witherspoon as an insanely driven high school student who aims to make her name in student politics, and Matthew Broderick as the teacher who stands in her way. A critical hit, it drew rave reviews for the performances of its cast, Witherspoon receiving a Golden Globe nomination and Payne an Oscar nod for Adapted Screenplay. *About Schmidt* starred Jack Nicholson as a recently retired man reflecting on his seemingly meaningless life as he travels across the country to the wedding of his only daughter. The film was a critical and financial success, and both Payne and Nicholson won Golden Globes for Adapted

Screenplay and Best Actor respectively. By the time Payne decided to make *Sideways* he had hit his stride and was the director for whom every actor in Hollywood would drop everything to 'take the call'. On paper, the movie doesn't look like much – two men in their forties take a week-long wine tasting trip to the Santa Barbara County Wine Country and encounter romance and adventures along the way – but it was a massive hit. It took nearly $110 million at the box office (from a budget of only $16 million) and picked up nominations from virtually every award ceremony that year. Owen Gleiberman at *Entertainment Weekly* described the film as 'the most exquisite American comedy since [Woody Allen's] *Annie Hall*'. It was nominated for five Oscars – winning Best Adapted Screenplay – and Payne and his main cast of actors received nominations and awards from the Golden Globes, BAFTA, the Directors Guild of America and swept the board at the Independent Spirit Awards (a ceremony that honours films made outside of Hollywood), where it won Best Film, Best Director, Best Screenplay and acting awards for its three main cast members.

It was a little surprising, then, that after *Sideways*, Payne wouldn't direct another film for seven years. In an article in *Entertainment Weekly*, Owen Gleiberman described him as 'the Stanley Kubrick of serious American comedy. He takes forever to make a movie, searching for the perfect book to adapt. But when he finally finds it and gets rolling, he turns each film into a fully realized inhabited universe unto itself'. The next 'universe' he was about to enter would be that of *The Descendants*.

He set about re-writing the original script with Jim Rash and Nat Faxon. What emerged was to become one of the most critically acclaimed films of 2011, and within it was the role that would cement Shailene Woodley's transition from television starlet to movie actress and, ultimately, change her life forever.

The initial round of auditions took place in Los Angeles while she was still scheduled to be on set shooting *Secret Life*. Unfortunately, the producers refused to give Shailene the time off she required to attend. Hearing rumours that every young actress worth their salt, including Kristen Stewart and Amanda Seyfried, was fighting for a chance to meet with Payne and were desperate to play Alex must have been very disheartening for Shailene. Yet she realized that antagonizing the producers of *Secret Life* would only lead to problems in the future, something her complicated life did not need. The film may have found its director, but as time went on it still hadn't found its Alex. Fortunately for Shailene, Payne had set up meetings to see more girls for the role, this time in New York. She eventually read for Payne by taking an overnight round trip from filming in Toronto to the audition.

Around the same time, it was rumoured that her on-screen partnership with Daren Kagasoff had blossomed into an off-screen romance. Thrown together for long hours in a high-pressure situation, it's no surprise that relationships would blossom. There was plenty to admire about Daren, as Brenda Hampton pointed out to EW.com. 'He's immensely talented, he's a hard worker, and he's a kind man.' She added, 'When we were on location, crowds of girls would find us and they'd scream his name with an enthusiasm not unlike that of girls meeting The Beatles at the airport.' She concluded, 'He's got "It", whatever "It" is, and he's got it in spades.' How could Shailene resist?

Thus, Shailene, in late 2009, shortly after she turned eighteen and during the extended break after the filming of series two of *Secret Life*, free from her studies and looking towards her future, decided with Daren that they were going to move to New York together. They took an apartment on the Lower East Side and both of them saw it chiefly as an adventure and an opportunity to explore acting roles outside of their *Secret Life* commitments and make some new contacts in the wider film and television industry. Proving her willingness to stand on her own two feet, as well as her well documented down-to-earth nature, Shailene took a job working for US high street clothing chain American Apparel. She was keen to remain as anonymous as possible, telling *BlackBook* magazine, 'None of my co-workers knew I was an actor. And thank God, because I didn't want them to know. There's such a weird, preconceived image of what an actor is, and I didn't want anyone to think of me like that.' And if anyone had the acting ability to pull it off, it was Shailene. Unfortunately, her secret wasn't going to stay under wraps for long.

It was on her second day working there that she got the call from her agent telling her Payne had loved her first audition and wanted to meet her for coffee to discuss the role of Alex. The problem was the meeting had to take place the next day, in Los Angeles, when Shailene was scheduled to be at work in New York. Talking to *BlackBook*, she explained how her agent had implored her to move heaven and earth to attend. 'He said, "Shai, you need to fly to LA tomorrow. Alexander wants to have coffee with you."'

Feeling she had made a pledge to her fellow workers, she had replied, 'I can't do that, it's my second day at American Apparel, I have a commitment, I can't let them down.' She begged them to allow her to set up the session via Skype, but Payne, understandably, insisted it had to be a face-to-face meeting. Her agent was adamant Shailene should make the trip. She remembers him pleading, 'Shailene, I never tell you to do anything, and I really believe you need to do this.' Knowing it was the right thing to do for her career, but with regret, she called in sick. She secretly booked a round trip from New York to LA, planning to be back at work the next day, mindful that she would still need a job if the meeting turned out to be a dead end. She met with Payne and as soon as it was over, Shailene took a taxi back to the airport.

Fortunately, the meeting went well and Payne was immediately taken with her. He undoubtedly picked up on Shailene's boundless energy, her inner strength and quiet and assured elegance. He was similarly impressed with the maturity and intelligence she displayed, qualities that unquestionably belied her tender age. He told *Entertainment Weekly*, 'I was looking for a seventeen-year-old Debra Winger – someone who had that same fire and the same vulnerability.' Winger was a beautiful young actress who had found fame, alongside Richard Gere, in the romantic drama *An Officer and a Gentleman* in the early 1980s. She was small and feminine, but had received acclaim (and an Oscar nomination) for her ability to bring an unexpected toughness and steely determination to her performances.

It was rumoured Payne had seen nearly three hundred girls for the role and was initially unsure about Shailene because he was looking for someone with little to no acting experience. A girl who could almost be described as an industry veteran, with an ongoing role in a major television series seemed like an unlikely choice, but Payne was quick to reconsider, he said to EW.com. 'About two minutes into her audition, my jaw was dropping open. I just thought, "This girl is going to be the one to beat."'

Shailene also remembered that although the meeting went well – 'he told me I was his number one choice' – it was far from over. Payne was obviously under a lot of pressure to cast the right type of actress, a key factor being her ability to believably portray a teenage girl who had been born and raised as a Hawaii native. She told *BlackBook* magazine, 'He was going to Hawaii [anyway], and he was going to audition every girl in Hawaii, and if there was one that was better suited for the role than me, he would call me and tell me personally that I did not [get the role].' The girl who had been born and raised in sunny California was resigned to her fate and accustomed to the politics of Hollywood. 'That to me was enough . . . I thought it was so respectful and honest of him to do that.' She was secure in the fact that she had done everything she could and went back to her sales assistant job at American Apparel.

Her career in retail, however, lasted longer than her relationship with Daren. She told 411Mania.com that earlier romantic experiences had been valuable in helping her understand what she was actually looking for in terms of the types of boys she was dating, saying, 'Most of my relationships have ended in a mature way . . . [me and Daren not working out] let me figure out more about myself and what I wanted in future relationships.'

When they split, Daren returned to California. True to the independent spirit she had always shown, Shailene stayed on in New York by herself, working at American Apparel for another month. Describing her time alone in New York to *Paper* magazine, all she had to say was, '[I] had a ball.' She only gave up her job at American Apparel when she eventually received the call from Payne, telling her she had got the role she was so hungry for – she had been cast as Alex in *The Descendants*. Her first reaction was to burst into tears: 'I bawled', she told *BlackBook* magazine.

Shailene was on hiatus from *Secret Life*, but she had to be back in Los Angeles to start filming season three in May 2010. Brenda

Hampton told EW.com, 'I was not surprised when her agent called asking if she could be released to co-star in a film with George Clooney.' She and the show's producers knew they couldn't keep their golden goose caged forever and allowed Shailene to take an extended four-month break from filming. The soon-to-be film star was used to her schedule being incredibly busy but this was going to be a tight squeeze.

Hampton related that it was not an unusual turn of events. 'We found a way to write the story to [accommodate Shailene's situation], as we do so many times in television.' As it turned out, Shailene wanting to leave the show for an extended period to make *The Descendants* became the jump-off point for her character Amy's fight for her own independence within the main storyline of the show. It was going to be tough, but if they all pulled together, they would make it work.

Having secured time off from filming *Secret Life*, Payne got all his principle actors together for a 'table read' of the script. This, as the name implies, involves the whole cast sitting around a large table in a rehearsal room and reading their lines aloud. Like an early run through for a play, it necessarily allows the writers and director to see which parts of the script are working and how the actors are 'fitting in to' their characters. As George Clooney himself is reported to have said, highlighting a read-through's importance, 'You can make a bad movie out of a good script, but you can't make a good movie out of a bad script.' The table read would be the first time Shailene would meet the man who was to play her on-screen father.

Dubbed 'sexiest man alive' by much of the press, George Clooney has risen slowly through the ranks of jobbing actors to join the Hollywood A-list, picking up Oscar nominations for acting (including a win for *Syriana* in 2005), producing (another win, for *Argo* in 2012), directing and writing – becoming the only other person apart from Walt Disney to receive nominations in six different Oscar categories. Barring a few missteps along the way, Clooney has settled into a pattern of delivering solid performances in an incredibly varied selection of thought-provoking political films, popcorn movies and multiplex fillers.

Shailene had only learned about his involvement after she had auditioned for the film, so the chance to work with an actor of his stature wasn't really a factor in her wanting the role. She was understandably thrilled but, she insisted, was not nervous about meeting him. She quipped to MoviesOnline.ca, 'It was exciting. It'd be like an artist going to meet Picasso. That's cool . . . right?'

The first sit-down read-through was at the LA Four Seasons Hotel. She told the *Hollywood Reporter*, 'I wasn't intimidated by working with George Clooney until I saw him, and my heart started pounding, and I was like, "Oh, that's George Clooney!" . . . Then he came over, and gave me a giant hug, and said "Welcome, sweetie!" Something really warm.' From then on, she felt at ease.

Clooney had always been Alexander Payne's number-one choice to play Matt King, the troubled husband and father at the centre of *The Descendants* story; perhaps the idea had been planted in his mind when he read the book – one character is described as wearing a T-shirt with the slogan 'MRS CLOONEY' emblazoned across it. It was instantly obvious the next few months were to be a complete revelation to Shailene, and she would look back on the experience as a truly life-changing, magical time.

Shailene had loved the original script and had gone even crazier for the re-write by Payne and his co-writers. She explained what it was about the story and the character of Alex she found so exciting in an interview with Collider.com: 'So often I read scripts and am like, "This would never happen in real life. It's not trying to be funny. It's trying to be serious." But this was real and it was messy, and I responded to it.' Not only was she working with the best script she had ever been given, she also had the original source novel to refer to. 'I did read the book . . . That was incredibly helpful because a screenplay is ninety pages and a book is three hundred, so it fills in the blanks. I did get that luxury on this film.'

Payne insisted his main cast and crew fly out to Hawaii for four weeks prior to the start of filming. He was convinced the actors would benefit from this spell together, allowing them to spend time bonding as a family group and, as Shailene explained to the *Hollywood Reporter*, the director also wanted them 'to get the vibe . . . because it's very different from anywhere else.' The mostly LA-based actors needed time to acclimatize to the Hawaiian way of life and to allow them to more truthfully portray a family who had spent their whole lives growing up there.

The minute she stepped off the plane, Shailene knew she was visiting somewhere very special. She told HollywoodChicago. com that it awakened something inside her and felt like a spiritual home: 'I had never been to Hawaii, and definitely my body was born in Los Angeles, but my heart is from Hawaii . . . it's a magical place, with a very strong energy, which grounded me, centred me and helped me listen to my heart instead of my mind.' Shailene felt a new freedom here, a place to escape from the frantic pace and negative elements of her LA lifestyle, which she had always endeavoured to reject. 'It basically allowed me to get out of the materialistic bubble with which we often surround ourselves,' adding with a laugh, 'There are more chickens there than people.'

The cast and crew moved around the island like a large extended family. Even after the acclimatizing pre-shoot period was over, they would spend the time they were not filming exploring the island. Shailene explained to *New York* magazine, 'We were hiking up waterfalls, jumping off things, kayaking, snorkelling, and doing things [as far as insurance is concerned] we probably shouldn't.' Even for a girl who had spent most of her life barefoot in trees and swimming in lakes, it truly was an adventure in paradise.

One of the key elements in creating a convincing Hawaiian family was finding the right look for the main cast. As George Clooney's character says in a voiceover early in the film to explain a room full of Hawaiian shirted men, 'Don't be fooled by appearances. In Hawaii, some of the most important people look like bums and stuntmen.' Alex, and therefore Shailene, had to look like a typical Hawaiian teenager. So, as part of their cultural exploration, they organized a few field trips to the island's shopping malls to see what the local girls were wearing. In close collaboration with costume designer Wendy Chuck, Shailene put together Alex's wardrobe. They agreed it had to be very basic, things normal girls could find at any mall. Thus, her wardrobe consisted mostly of T-shirts and cut-off jeans. Shailene had also noticed virtually every girl she had seen had an ankle bracelet on, so, for Alex, they tied a small piece of hemp around her ankle for every scene.

From her earliest readings of the script, Shailene had been more than a little surprised that Alex was described as wearing a bikini in a lot of scenes. She told MoviesOnline about her first reaction, 'I'm freaking out!' she cried. Her fears were soon put to rest, as, she continued, 'once you're there, everyone is in a bikini. You go to a gas station and they're filling up their cars in bikinis. You go to Foodland and they're walking around barefoot in bikinis and swim trunks.' She finished with a chuckle, 'You feel weird when you have clothes on there.'

The Descendants opens twenty-three days after Elizabeth King has been seriously hurt and left in a coma after a speedboat accident. Her husband, Matt, must keep it together for his two daughters, seventeen-year-old Alex and ten-year-old Scottie, as his life seems to be falling apart around him. Matt and his extended family are the owners of a large area of Hawaiian coastline, but, due to new ownership laws regarding inherited land in Hawaii, the family is forced to make a decision about who they sell it to before they lose the rights to own it outright themselves.

Matt works as a lawyer and has been instrumental in setting up the sale of the land as well as acting as the executor with the casting vote. With all of this going on, he realizes he has distanced himself from his family. The doctors tell Matt that Elizabeth is not responding to any treatment and there is nothing more they can do, so Matt should take the time to start preparing everyone for the inevitable.

We first see Shailene as Alex, out after curfew, hitting golf balls around the playing fields behind her school. She is obviously drunk and is obnoxious and rude to her father. Matt asks himself, 'What is it that makes the women in my life want to destroy themselves? Elizabeth with her motorcycles and speed boats and drinking and Alex with her drugs and older men.'

The next scene is Shailene's first important scene of the film. Alex is in the family swimming pool when Matt tells her the truth about her mother's condition. They 'are letting her go'. The realization that slowly crosses her face is a devastating mix of fear and sorrow as she is forced to accept the harsh reality of the situation. She slips under the water as she breaks down over the news.

Alex decides to help her father, but she is still being difficult. She introduces him to Sid, a boy she went to school with. Sid is a bit of a 'stoner' and Alex's relationship with him is obviously a weapon in her fight to hurt her father. They visit Elizabeth in hospital. This is the first time Alex has seen the rapid deterioration of her mother. She starts to apologize to her, but it turns into an attack. Matt is angry and tells her not to spoil the memory of her mother for Scottie. As she calms down, she tells her mother, 'I'm exactly like you'. Alex then reveals to her father that she found out her mother was having an affair with another man, months before the accident. They bond over this secret and when Matt decides to take a trip to one of the other islands to track down Brian Speer, Elizabeth's lover, Alex insists the whole family, and Sid, tag along. In their travels around the island, we see the family unit grow closer as they share memories of Elizabeth.

In another of Shailene's key scenes, Matt complains about the way Alex swears in front of him, stating, 'The way you talk around me . . . you don't respect authority.' From the look on Shailene's face, we understand that she does not consider Matt to be the authority figure he thinks he should be.

Matt finally tracks down Brian Speer and meets his wife and two young sons. He finds out Speer is an estate agent and is working for the local bidder who is trying to buy Matt's family's land. He realizes Speer will benefit financially if they decide to go with the local bid. He and Alex use this as a way to visit Brian and offer him the chance to see Elizabeth in the hospital and pay his respects before she dies. This is a particularly interesting scene for Shailene; we see a light comedic side to her performance that she hadn't really had the chance to show before.

The family return home and must now face the fact that Elizabeth is dying. Both girls begin to expose their more vulnerable sides and drop the front they have built to protect themselves, and Matt is now in a position to be a father to both of them. In one of Shailene's final scenes, she defends Matt against verbal attacks from Elizabeth's father.

The day of the land sale vote arrives and goes in favour of the local bid. Matt defies the majority and decides they will not sell the land. They will spend the seven years they have before the law changes working out a way to keep the land within the family and benefit the whole of Hawaii. They lead privileged lives and keep the true Hawaii at arm's length, saying, 'But we've got Hawaiian blood and we're tied to the land . . . and our children are tied to the land.'

Elizabeth dies and he and his children say their goodbyes, scattering Elizabeth's ashes in the sea off the coast of the island. The last scene opens with Scottie curled up on the sofa watching *March of the Penguins*. Matt comes into the room with two bowls of ice cream and he sits beside his daughter. He pulls a blanket over them and they start to eat. Alex enters from the back of the room and joins her family on the sofa. She slips under the blanket and Matt hands her his bowl of ice cream. The family are reunited. It may not exactly be a happy ending, but we are left with the feeling that there is hope for them as a united family, better equipped to face the future together.

Shailene had fought hard to be a part of the film. Keen to get away from playing high school students (she would be turning nineteen in a few months), she relished the chance to show off the comedic side of her acting talent in a more nuanced and demanding performance. She was especially thrilled to get the chance to play a character like Alex, a young woman who was at such an intense crossroads in her life. Shailene was quick to point out to *BlackBook* that, although she was nothing like Alex – 'I'm not her. I didn't do drugs in high school and I don't drink, and I'm not bitchy like she is' – she understood where she was coming from as a character. 'I think everyone has a pain and a bitch [inside] them. I don't often use that side of myself because I really don't have reason to.'

Alex had some very difficult decisions to make about who she was and the part she had to play in the lives of the people around her. She had protected herself from the abandonment she thought she had suffered at the hands of her parents by lashing out and being abrupt and rude. She had made her own choices in life, but it is a false independence that she was emotionally ill-equipped to handle. She is forced to evolve rapidly to deal with some new realities and in the process she softens and admits she really does need the protection of a father.

Shailene told the *Huffington Post* she believed Alex was 'going through the most angsty periods in her life, [she] thought the world was out to get her; kind of took on the victim thing'. She continued, 'I think she created such a barrier, such a wall around her that she never was really forced to examine her life, and the consequences of her relationships.' Shailene describes how, as events unfold in the movie, Alex must gather all her inner strength, saying, 'In the end, she's become vulnerable,' a state that allows her to open up to her father and gives her the opportunity to turn her life around, put some of her darkness behind her and begin again. Shailene concluded, 'She has a chance to not only reconnect with her family but reconnect with herself.'

Shailene's approach to acting is refreshingly simple. She believes she should be able to find most of what she needs to bring a character to life in the script – even better if it's adapted from a source novel – which cuts down the need for too much extra research or 'method' acting. 'I do zero research . . . unless it's a period piece,' she told Collider.com, her theory being that actors have little or no control over what actually happens when they get onto a movie set. Any preconceived ideas about how a scene will play out, or how a character will react in any given situation will inevitably disappear out of the window as soon as the cameras roll. The best an actor can do is show up with all their lines memorized and then feed off what happens within the scene, with the other actors adding their own flavour to the situation. Truthful emotion will be triggered naturally by the words on the page, mixed with the actors interacting on set.

She told the *Boston Phoenix* in typically modest terms, 'I'm not a good actor. I'm just a professional listener. If you listen to the words, if you listen to the truth of a moment [in the script], you'll react truthfully.' She went on to succinctly describe it, saying, 'For me, it's not about developing a character or researching a character or being a character, it's about being myself within the rules and restrictions of a specific character.' She concluded that in this case, 'I was Shailene through Alexandra's mouth.'

When asked about which scenes she found hardest, she told Collider.com, 'From a very humble point of view, there weren't any hard scenes to film because we had such a brilliant screenplay. There wasn't a lot of guessing for us to do as actors.' Refreshingly self-effacing as always, but the truth is that Shailene had become such an accomplished performer, so at ease in front of the camera, she may not have fully realized the important contribution she was making to the film.

The first of Shailene's key scenes sees Matt confide in Alex, telling her that her mother is not going to recover from the coma and, as per her wishes, they are not going to try to keep her alive artificially. The scene takes place with Alex in the family's outdoor swimming pool. When this devastating news starts to sink in, we see Alex hit by a wave of grief. She disappears under the water and the camera follows her. We view her sobbing and obviously distressed.

She told *New York* magazine it was one of the scenes that had first attracted her to the script. 'It was selfishly my own therapy session. I got to scream underwater. I just naturally cried because if you were being told that [about] your mom, you would cry in real life.' In another interview, with the *Hollywood Reporter*, Shailene described just how much of this scene came from her own interpretation of the script. 'The script said, "She goes under water and distorts her face" . . . the water has always been [my] safe zone. So it was really exciting for me to take [Alex] who had just heard this awful news about her mother, and to be able to escape into the water . . . it was like a baby in a womb – no-one can hear you, you can be vulnerable and nobody knows.'

She elaborated on this idea to MoviesOnline. 'In Hawaii, there's a saying that Hawaiians learn to swim before they learn to walk, and so I thought it was really beautiful that upon hearing such tragic news she would recede in to the water, into her comfort zone.'

Shailene pointed out that she only did four takes of the

swimming pool scene, with director Alexander Payne insisting he was keen to capture the spontaneity of the sequence, keeping it fresh and real. While the shots of Shailene distressed and sobbing in anguish underwater are undoubtedly powerful, the scene's real emotional clout begins as soon as she hears the news. Shailene instantly manages to convey the crushing blow of fear and disappointment in Alex's face as the realization that her mother is gone forever drains the youthful arrogance from her and she starts to cry.

The next major scene for Shailene is when her character has to tell her father that she knew about the affair her mother was having before her accident. She explains that she had confronted her mother about it during her last visit home and they had argued. Her grief is further compounded by the fact that this confrontation was never resolved as she hadn't spoken to her mother for a long time before her accident. These words, exchanged in anger, might be the last conversation they would ever have. At first she is angry with her father, but it soon turns to pity when she realizes he was completely oblivious to the affair. Shailene manages to show a wide range of emotions within this scene. She is defiant with regards to her unresolved issues with her mother and manages to express both frustrated anger and then, ultimately, sympathy towards her father.

Finding 'the truth' inside the character of Alex wasn't the only challenge she was facing. This was the first time she had found herself working with a director of Alexander Payne's calibre. But she would quickly understand any insecurities she might have had about her abilities were unfounded. She was in this film because Payne had handpicked her from a very long list of exceptionally talented young actresses. He told the *Los Angeles Times*, 'She has a remarkably good head on her shoulders . . . clever, compassionate, perceptive . . . and she has been well parented.' These were the key qualities he knew would bring Alex to life. The audition process had been a long one for good reason. He was quick to tell all his actors, 'I hired you to be you.'

When filming began, Shailene took some time to get used to Payne's style of working and the general tone of the film, she told the *Huffington Post*. 'Truly, I didn't know if we were making a comedy or a drama.' She explained that although Payne famously didn't insist on his actors doing multiple takes of the same scenes, aiming instead to capture natural, unrehearsed reactions, his method did encourage experimentation within these few takes. 'We would do one scene one way and then do it another way.' Confusing at first, she began to catch on quickly. She continued, 'It was just Alexander going, "Okay, now instead of glaring, why don't you smile?" And you're like, "What? That makes no sense!"'

She soon appreciated that Payne came to the movie with a very strong idea of the tone he was after and what he wanted the finished movie to be. His confidence had a knock-on effect with his actors. By accepting and adopting the processes that were instrumental to the director's previous successes, she was becoming a better, more intuitive actor. She understood as soon as she saw the playback of her first scenes and could see the different shades it was giving her performance.

She was struck by Payne's use of positive reinforcement, she told MoviesOnline. 'If you're doing something he loves, he'll actually give you [praise]', a very different approach to her experiences on the set of *Secret Life*. She went on, 'No one ever tells you when you're doing good. Generally, they just point out when you're doing not so great.' She quickly realized she had been given the opportunity of a lifetime – to learn her craft from a true master, and she was determined not to squander a second of it. She described it to *Paper* magazine as like being in a playground: 'You can try the slide for a few minutes, then you play on the swings. He gives you the chance to explore yourself and to be yourself.'

Payne was also eager to educate Shailene about cinema – she had admitted she was 'uneducated' when it came to knowing specific producers, writers, directors and actors. Payne supplied her with a long list of his recommended films, including *The Apartment*, *The Graduate* and *Annie Hall*. Her lack of knowledge extended to Payne's output as well. She told several interviewers she had seen *Sideways* with her parents when she was about fourteen and had spent the entire film wondering why they were laughing so much. She re-visited the film after she signed on to *The Descendants*, finally old enough to understand the subtleties of the humour.

Working with Alexander Payne was to have a long-lasting and profound effect on Shailene. Long after filming had ended, she would describe his methods, and the personal acting awakening it had prompted, to the *Los Angeles Times*. 'He's the shore of the river, and we are the water. He gives us the freedom to create whatever currents we want, [hitting] whatever rocks we want, but within the rules and boundaries of [his] vision.' She went on to reveal, 'Alexander became, and continues to be, one of my top five favourite human beings on the planet. He is a magical man . . . Just from getting to know him as a spiritual, artistic, creative and spectacular human being, I really learned more about myself.'

Shailene was on familiar ground when it came to dealing with the relationships she had to build with the other members of the cast. She had spent the last couple of years forming strong working bonds and many close friendships on the *Secret Life* set.

Nick Krause played Alex's 'almost' boyfriend, Sid, in the film. It's fairly obvious from the start of the film that Alex is only hanging out with Sid to annoy her father; he is definitely not the smartest of people. Krause was fairly new to screen acting – although he may have crossed paths with Shailene when they both appeared in episodes of the 'young' Kennedy brothers TV drama, *Jack and Bobby*, in 2004 – but he had a solid background in improvised comedy, which is used to good effect in *The Descendants*. He is incredibly bright and had started taking college classes at the age of ten.

Shailene and Nick are the same age but were brought up in very different environments (California and Texas respectively), but they found they did have a lot in common. They both had a lifelong love of the outdoors and spent a lot of time exploring the island together. Shailene told Collider.com, 'We had a lot to teach each other, and a lot to learn from each other . . . My bonding with Nick was a very organic process. We became like brother and sister.'

Initially, Shailene had some doubts about Nick's casting – she had envisioned him to be tall and awkward – and she didn't think he fitted her mental image of Sid's character. Clearly, Shailene should have trusted Payne's immaculate casting technique as, soon enough, she found herself impressed with Nick's ability to transform himself, she told MoviesOnline. 'He's brilliant . . . In real life he has an IQ off the charts . . . an incredible genius, but you would never know that because in the movie he acts like a really good stoner.'

The actress who had been picked to play Alex's ten-year-old-sister, Scottie, was Amara Miller. *The Descendants* was Amara's acting debut, never having even appeared in a school play. She had come to the attention of Alexander Payne as the child of a friend of a friend and was cast less than a fortnight before shooting started. Payne was determined to get a completely natural performance from her, which caused some problems for the other actors. Shailene told MoviesOnline, 'Who you see on screen is just so authentically her . . . We'd be doing a scene and she'd start swinging her arms around, and at first I'd go, "Oh my gosh, we're filming a scene. Stop doing that", [but] sometimes it would work.' She re-affirmed this in an interview with Collider.com: 'It worked because she wasn't jaded . . . she's incredible, and we bonded very quickly.' To Shailene, 'Nick, Amara and I just became a little family.'

During filming, her relationship with George Clooney developed into something very special. In an interview with Collider.com she described him as 'Superhuman . . . that's the only word I can use that will truly encompass everything about him.' She told Moviefone.com they had quickly settled into a comfortable groove. 'He's not George Clooney, "famous man", to me anymore. He's George Clooney, guy from Kentucky . . . just a good guy.' She continued praising him for his down-to-earth nature and for not being stand-offish or disappearing into his trailer when he wasn't shooting his scenes. Instead, he would be on set, observing and helping the young actors with their scenes. 'He's just amazing . . . I have never met a more generous, philanthropic human being in my entire life . . . he will do anything for you. There are small things that he does on a daily basis, for anyone and everyone, that just blew me away.'

Shailene had to film several intense scenes of conflict with Clooney, involving a lot of arguing and swearing, which she described as an especially enjoyable challenge. 'It's fun! In most movies they're like, "Oh, no, no. We need it to be [family friendly]. We can't say that."' She particularly enjoyed sparring with Clooney: 'to be able to [swear] to an actor like George Clooney, who can spit right back at you . . . I love arguing. I always say that I'll never win a physical battle, but I can always win a mental battle.'

Her director would also compliment her on her ability to face-off against heavyweight actors like Clooney, saying to the *Los Angeles Times*, 'That's part of her talent and maturity . . . she can hold her own in any situation . . . she's the real McCoy.'

Aside from the swearing, her Clooney education also extended to him teaching her how to 'play drunk' for a scene – the key thing being to act as if you don't actually think you are drunk. It's probably just as well that Shailene had already come through her own (brief) rebellious phase.

She appreciated how lucky she was to be working with an actor of this calibre – considered to be one of the best in the world – in her first big movie. She knew it would test her and force her to use every skill she had to meet the challenge. She told MovieOnline, 'I got to rise to this awesome occasion and raise the stakes, and I had to be on top of my game and be so incredibly professional and ready to be there.' She was especially keen to separate Clooney 'the movie star' from who he was as an actor and as a man away from the camera. 'He is just so normal and so human, [but] talk about a professional! He is a great actor because he's a great actor, not because an editor makes him look good.'

When asked by *New York* magazine about her relationship with George Clooney, she said, 'A crush on George? He's fifty!' She went on to explain, 'I guess I have a crush on him in terms of him just being a phenomenal human being . . . I'm enamoured by his human being-ness, and who he is in this world.' She concluded with a laugh, 'But no, he's fifty. That would be weird to say I had a crush on him . . . I'm just turning twenty.' It seems Shailene still had a lot to learn about what goes on in Hollywood!

Clooney, famous for his on-set pranks, was forced to tone it down a bit – Amara Miller, who was playing Scottie, the youngest member of the King family was, after all, only ten years-old when filming took place – but Shailene recalled how he would surprise everyone with the 'fart app' on his phone and reduce the younger (and some of the older) members of the cast to fits of giggles. 'He has this amazing ability to be goofy and silly, and in the blink of an eye transform into the vulnerable, serious character.'

Working with George Clooney was to teach her many things about the craft of acting and what she could achieve, not only in terms of her career, but as a spokesperson, someone given a platform via the attention they received for their acting abilities. It was this lesson, coupled with the obvious connection she now had with Hawaii, its people and their unique spirit that may have had the deepest and longest-lasting impact on Shailene.

George Clooney was quoted in *Entertainment Weekly* as saying, '[Shailene's] talents are underused and underappreciated on this TV show she's on.' His words must have been ringing in her ears when, still riding high on the experience of filming *The Descendants*, with at least two years still left on her contract, Shailene returned to her 'day job' on the set of *Secret Life* in the late Spring of 2010. Brenda Hampton, the show's creator, announced the series would definitely return with Shailene on board, telling EW.com, 'She wants to stay with the show. Doing [*The Descendants*] was a very good thing for her and for us. She brought what she learned back.'

(Left) Starting point: Shailene in one of her earliest roles in *A Place Called Home*, 2004.

(Above) Looking angelic as the titular character in *Felicity: An American Adventure*, 2005.

(*Above left*) Shailene attends the official opening of the American Girl store in Los Angeles in 2006.
(*Above right; below*) Secret to success: the first step on her road to fame and fortune, Shailene is cast as pregnant teenager Amy Juergens in *The Secret Life of the American Teenager*, pictured with the cast.

(Top left; above) Shailene quickly learned to play the part of experienced actress as she helps promote *Secret Life* in 2009.

(Left) Shailene poses for the first of many red carpet snaps as she attends the 2009 Teen Choice Awards, where she was nominated for Choice TV Actress in a Drama.

(*Above*) Star quality: Theo with the cast of *Bedlam*. (*l–r*) Will Young, Charlotte Salt, Theo, Ashley Madekwe, Hugo Speer.

(*Below*) Theo's charm wows the audience during the *Bedlam* panel at the Summer Television Critics Association Tour in Beverly Hills, 2011.

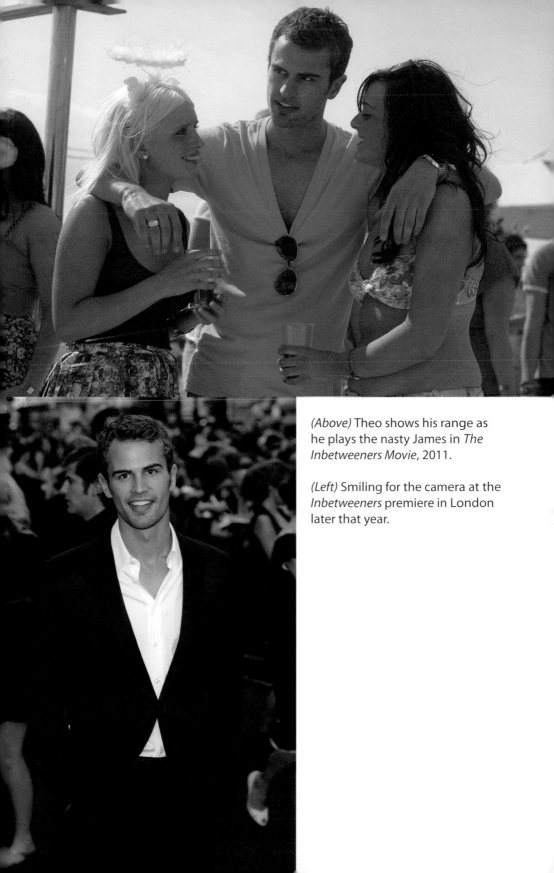

(Above) Theo shows his range as he plays the nasty James in *The Inbetweeners Movie*, 2011.

(Left) Smiling for the camera at the *Inbetweeners* premiere in London later that year.

(Above; right) Going places: Shailene with her co-stars in what would be her biggest break yet, *The Descendants.*

(Below) With (*l–r*) Director Alexander Payne, George Clooney, Amara Miller and Nick Krause, 2011.

(Above left; below) Theo would also shine in his biggest movie to date, as vampire David in *Underworld: Awakening.*
(Above right) Getting along famously: Theo and co-star Kate Beckinsale enjoy a moment at the LA premiere of the film in 2012.

(*Top right*) Shailene and George Clooney have fun at the 2011 Toronto International Film Festival, where *The Descendants* would secure a distribution deal with Fox Searchlight.

(*Above; right*) Shailene, Nick Krause and on-screen sister Amara Miller shared a great relationship long after the cameras stopped rolling.

In the same article Shailene is also quoted, putting her trademark optimistic spin on things, and re-emphasizing her commitment and love for the show. 'The storylines change often, so [there are] a lot of different colours to explore.'

The truth was, before filming *The Descendants*, Shailene had become increasingly frustrated with the busy schedule, long shooting days and the 'production-line' approach to making a television show, she told EW.com at a later date. 'Time is of the essence and money is of the essence [when making a TV show], so it's very uncreative on a lot of levels.'

But something had changed. As frustrated as she was with the restrictions it placed on her, Shailene's attitude towards *Secret Life* had begun to mellow since making the film. Her hunger to explore outside opportunities seemed to be temporarily satisfied. Maybe it was the laid-back attitude of the Hawaiian people that had rubbed off on her, or could it be she had been lucky enough to receive some sage advice from her *Descendants* mentor, George Clooney? It's easy to forget that before Clooney became the A-list movie star we know him as today, he was a bit-part actor struggling to find work in Hollywood until he got his big break, in what would be a five-year run on hospital drama *ER* at the ripe old age of thirty-three. An example such as his might have reminded her to slow down and not be in too much of a rush to experience everything at once. She wouldn't be tied to the show forever and there would be plenty of time to enjoy the success *Secret Life* had afforded her when her contract was over.

Shailene had successfully made the transition from television to the big screen. She told Collider.com, 'It felt like just going to a different school. You don't really notice the transition when you're in the moment.' She went on to explain, 'I like diving into the character for a few months, and then leaving it behind.' She had resigned herself to the fact that she would not be leaving Amy Juergens behind for quite a while and she would indeed be returning to the show, but equally, she wanted everyone to know movies were now where her heart was. It's easy to speculate that the praise she had received for her performance in *The Descendants* gave her a newfound confidence to relax, reassured she did have what it takes to become another character apart from Amy, and prove to everyone she could inhabit new, relatable and emotionally genuine roles.

Whatever it was, she played out the next two years of her *Secret Life* contract without taking on any major extra-curricular film or television work. It is reported that it was during this time that Shailene had ruled herself out of the running to play Katniss Everdeen in the forthcoming film adaptation of *The Hunger Games* – a role which virtually every actress between the ages of fifteen and twenty-five had been desperate to audition for. She told MTV, 'Yeah, I definitely auditioned. It wasn't, like, a great audition. But I think Jennifer Lawrence is perfect for the role.' It would be this role that would ultimately turn Jennifer Lawrence into a genuine movie star and transform her into Hollywood royalty. It seemed Shailene had decided to revisit the initial promise she'd made to her mother – she would only continue acting if she was still having fun doing it.

Fun, it appeared, was definitely now her main priority. It was during this time she appeared in a music video for one of her favourite bands, Best Coast. Commissioned as a ten-minute MTV 'Supervideo' and directed by Drew Barrymore (someone who was well aware of the pressures of being a child star), the promo clip for 'Our Deal' featured several of Hollywood's hottest rising young stars in a twisted, dream-like homage to *The Warriors* and *West Side Story*. Besides Shailene, it also featured Chloë Moretz, Tyler Posey, Miranda Cosgrove and Alia Shawkat.

She also found time to use her regular August hiatus from *Secret Life* to fulfil her lifelong dream of backpacking around Europe with one of her best girlfriends. Speaking to the *Los Angeles Times*, she said, 'Everything was so spontaneous.' Truly an eye-opening experience, she found herself exposed to amazing sights and sounds travelling through Spain, France and Italy. They stayed in youth hostels and sometimes ended up taking overnight, cross-country journeys, sleeping on the trains and meeting some wonderfully 'exotic' fellow travellers along the way. Shailene recalled, 'At one point, a guy who was tripping on drugs sat down next to us on the train. He spoke six languages and knew more about US politics than I did. It was unnerving, but also kind of great.' She told the *Boston Phoenix* she'd even called in a favour from her on-screen dad, George Clooney, and stopped by his Italian villa for a refuel and pamper. 'I showed up at his house with my friend and a giant backpack and dirty shoes and I was like, "Can I borrow your laundry machine, 'cause our clothes are dirty!"'

She got a taste for real Italian culture, their general outlook on life and, in particular, the abundance and freshness of their food. It was an incredible experience for Shailene, a welcome break from her busy routine, and it would allow her to recharge her batteries and refocus. She told *The Lab*, 'It was magnificent and amazing. And I would do it again in a heartbeat.'

Meanwhile, Alexander Payne had been working tirelessly on *The Descendants* since location filming had wrapped up in May 2010. Once the process of putting the film together was complete, it was time to let everyone else see the end results. It was clear this was a special film and, as such, its journey out into the cutthroat world of film distribution had to be orchestrated perfectly. Payne knew that even with George Clooney aboard, he had made a film that would struggle to be heard above the crash and bang of the typical Hollywood blockbuster. The film had 'award season' written all over it.

Award season films are generally considered to be small- or mid-budget films aimed at an older audience, such as book adaptations or character studies. They are released towards the end of the year, after the last summer blockbuster has finished its run, just in time to remain fresh in the minds of the key award voting panels. The best way to get blanket coverage for these films is to send them out on the film festival circuit. If a film has been made independently of the main studios, this is where distribution deals are signed and sealed. They will be seen by the world's cinema elite and reviewed months in advance of mainstream release, starting the buzz that can be deafening by the time the Golden Globe and Oscar winners are announced.

This was another new experience for Shailene. She was in attendance for the red carpet duties when *The Descendants* previewed at the Telluride Film Festival in Colorado in early September 2011. The critical response was incredible. The film moved quickly to the Toronto Film Festival for its official debut. Owen Gleiberman of EW.com reviewed the film the day after it was shown, saying, '*The Descendants* is another beautifully chiselled gem – sharp, funny, generous, moving . . . watching this movie click together in its own brittle, original fashion is a richly satisfying experience.'

It was apparent that it wasn't just George Clooney who was

going to be picking up heat from the film. Gleiberman said, 'You're going to be hearing a lot about [Shailene Woodley] . . . she makes the teenage Alexandra such a sharp, beguiling presence that she seems to wash away the residue of a thousand bogus movie adolescents.' This was the role that was finally going to catapult Shailene into the big leagues. The film had picked up a distribution deal with Fox Searchlight at Toronto and continued on its critical roll-out as it moved on to the New York Film Festival.

The movie was scheduled for its US cinema release on 16 December 2011, but the overwhelming positive feedback it had received meant the distributors were keen to bring the release date forward a few weeks and begin a 'platform' release strategy. Because the US is such a large country, independent and art house films are often released on a small number of cinema screens, usually in LA and New York, and then expanded into more screens nationwide as word of mouth spreads. This would hopefully create a 'sleeper hit' (the box office returns growing gradually over an extended cinema run, rather than a huge advertising blitz that delivered a number-one movie in its first weekend) – indeed, it was a strategy that had worked for Payne before with *Sideways*. *The Descendants* officially began its US cinema run on 18 November 2011.

The staggered release also gave Shailene the chance to tour the country doing press and media interviews to promote the film in different cities as the picture was released. She enjoyed the chance to talk about a movie she was very proud of and to travel, seeing some of these places for the first time – even if, as she pointed out to *Time Out Chicago*, 'I don't have time to explore the cities . . . I get to see them through windows.' As the film's release began to expand, so did the praise for the film, and for

Shailene in particular.

The New York Times described Shailene's performance as 'one of the most insightful and unaffected depictions of a real American teenager in recent memory', while Peter Debruge said in his *Variety* review, '[Shailene] is a revelation in the role of Alex, displaying both the edge and depth the role demands.'

Shailene played down the praise she was receiving, telling the *Ventura County Star*, 'It's surreal. It's bizarre to read positive words about you that others wrote or said.' She would sum up *The Descendants* rollercoaster experience to the *Huffington Post* by saying, 'the audition was the cake, the performance in Hawaii was the icing on the cake, and [the acclaim and awards are] twenty jars of maraschino cherries'. She continued in a typically modest tone, not wanting to get her hopes up. 'I'm just taking it all in [my] stride and waking up every day with a smile on my face and in gratitude for what that day holds. And I have zero expectations; whatever happens, happens. It's beautiful either way, so I'm enjoying every moment and so grateful for every moment.'

Now the awards buzz was reaching fever pitch. *Rolling Stone* magazine said, 'Dynamite is the word for Woodley, who deserves to join Clooney and the movie on the march to awards glory.' The film was picking up nominations across the board and it was obvious there would be a lot of awards ceremonies to attend in the next few months. The festivals and press tours had quietened some of Shailene's nerves and she looked forward to the process and the prospect of meeting up with *The Descendants* family again. In an interview with *Malibu* magazine she said, 'I'm so fortunate to be with [the rest of the cast and crew]. They've been through this before, and they handle it with such grace'. She continued,

'It's really exciting, the awards season . . . I don't find it nerve racking; I don't find it overwhelming – I think because I've chosen to be myself within the process.'

In mid-November, Shailene attended the Governors Awards, an event hosted by the Academy of Motion Picture Arts and Sciences, which takes place prior to the Oscar nominee announcement, and where honorary awards are handed out in the presence of many of that year's potential nominees. Shailene was invited along to represent *The Descendants* and it acted as a fitting celebratory climax to the journey she had taken with the film. In the end, Shailene was frustratingly overlooked by the Academy Awards and had to settle for celebrating the nominations for George Clooney, Alexander Payne and the movie itself.

Shailene was very excited to be able to attend the Oscar ceremony, however, and once again reunite with *The Descendants* cast and crew. She chose to wear a full-length white Valentino couture dress, with a high neckline and small cut-away detailing on the front, which she described as 'so incredibly me'. While the dress is undoubtedly stunning, many criticised Shailene for dressing 'too old' and described the dress as being a bit 'stuffy'. In her red carpet interview for E! Online she told Ryan Seacrest, 'I love that it's long sleeved and classy and simple . . . I'm obsessed with it.' She told *ASOS* magazine after the event, 'A lot of people didn't like it. They were like, "She's twenty, she's covering herself up". But to me it felt classy and elegant and that's what I think of when I think of the Oscars.'

What is certain is Shailene looked very happy and relaxed. By staying covered up, she set herself apart from many of the other starlets walking the red carpet that night and stayed true to her principles. She concluded, 'I didn't do *The Descendants* to wear a designer's dress and a lot of make-up and get points from the fashion police.'

That night, the film would take home the Oscar for Best Adapted Screenplay. *The Descendants* would lose out in most of the major categories to another film which had debuted at the Toronto Film Festival, which Shailene herself had seen there and said she 'fell in love with': the silent, black and white movie, *The Artist*.

The film and its cast and crew did, however, pick up nominations from countless important industry awards panels, including the Gotham Awards (honouring achievement in films produced outside of the major studio system), the Screen Actors Guild, the Independent Spirit Awards, Critics' Choice as well as the Golden Globes. The film also made a solid showing at the BAFTAs. It picked up several awards including Movie of the Year from the American Film Institute, a Golden Globe and the Critics' Choice Award for Clooney, as well as several Best Screenplay gongs from the Satellite Awards, New York Film Critics Online, Independent Spirit and the National Board of Review.

The film cost approximately $20 million dollars to make and the worldwide box office would eventually exceed $175 million. Not bad for a small independent film about how tragedy can pull apart, and ultimately rebuild, a family.

Shailene picked up over forty different nominations for her performance in the film. She eventually won more than fifteen awards for her acting or as a member of the ensemble cast, including the Best Supporting Actress award at the Independent Spirit Awards and Breakthrough Performance at the MTV Movie Awards. It was obviously gratifying to receive positive reactions and acclaim for her work, but the whole experience had changed her in more profound ways. It had given her a new outlook on life. She had become an even more calm and focused person who was willing to sit back and enjoy the amazing things that were happening to her, but, as well as this, it had also opened her eyes to the larger problems faced by others less fortunate than herself. It had crystallized her already long-held views on the preservation of the environment, the struggles of indigenous people for the land that was rightfully theirs and re-enforced the importance of helping others understand these grander issues. She had begun to realize, because of her job and the positions it placed her in, that she had been given a voice and a platform to help educate others and bring about change.

Chapter Six

THEO: A HOLLYWOOD AWAKENING

THEO WAS ON THE MOVE. He was heading to Vancouver in Canada to start filming his first major Hollywood film, *Underworld: Awakening*, the fourth instalment in the popular vampire and werewolf saga. The films tell the story of a centuries-old feud between the vampire clans and their former slaves, the werewolves – also known as Lycans – a power struggle that rages while their existence remains hidden from the world's human population.

The franchise started as the brainchild of filmmaker Len Wiseman. Wiseman's career began as a music video and commercials director before he turned his attention to movies, entering the *Underworld* universe in 2003, when he co-created and directed the first film. It was while making *Underworld* that Wiseman met and began dating the film's lead actress, Kate Beckinsale. The pair would eventually marry in May 2004. The original film was savaged by critics, but enjoyed solid box office results internationally and managed to build enough of a cult following to ensure a sequel, *Underworld: Evolution*, which was released in 2006 and was also directed by Wiseman and starred

Beckinsale. Wiseman had demonstrated he was not only capable of creating an immersive and visually exciting new world, but he'd also shown the required stamina and strength to manage a major, special effects-driven, big-budget production. His involvement with the next two films was limited to a producer's role as he moved on to direct other projects, including *Die Hard 4.0* and the 2012 remake of *Total Recall*, starring Colin Farrell and – employing a hint of nepotism – Kate Beckinsale.

The *Underworld* franchise rolled on with a third instalment, *Underworld: Rise of the Lycans*, acting as a prequel to the previous two films. However, it undoubtedly suffered from the lack of Wiseman and Beckinsale's involvement. It was something of a surprise then when, in early 2011, it was announced the *Underworld* series was alive and well and a fourth movie would be released in early 2012. Although Wiseman was still absent from the director's chair – that duty would be split between Swedish filmmakers Måns Mårlind and Björn Stein – Beckinsale was returning to the franchise, reprising her role as Selene.

The film picked up where *Evolution* left off, with the humans now asserting their dominance over the newly revealed supernatural clans and Selene captured and held in suspended animation for scientific research. The action then skips forward twelve years to reveal a world where vampires and werewolves have been almost completely eradicated, forced underground by the humans and it is up to Selene to free herself and lead the fight, this time against mankind.

Theo's character is David, a vampire and the son of the coven leader. He represents a new, more rebellious breed of vampire. Tired of hiding in the shadows, he wishes to re-assert his clan's dominance over the humans who hunt them. This was certainly a very different role for the classically trained Theo. He threw himself into playing a convincing vampire, telling the Assignment X website, 'I think there's an animal in them', but, keen to show off his theatre school background and loftier ambitions for the role, he compared his character's situation to that of Caliban, a character who is forced into slavery in William Shakespeare's play *The Tempest*.

Theo's preparation involved taking advice from series veteran Kate Beckinsale. He said in an interview on the DVD bonus features, 'She is so embedded in the world. It has been useful, with little pointers when we're doing stuff – remembering the history, remembering the limits of the vampire, what they can do and what they can't.'

Theo told Upcoming-movies.com that although he had seen the first movie when it was released, he hadn't seen the others until he had been given the role in *Awakening*. 'What I like about the *Underworld* thing is that mix of cool genres, as well as creating its own message . . . it's also very dark, and it's quite badass.' It was definitely going to be a fun ride and there would be many challenges ahead. Most of those were going to be physical, and Theo was keen to take advantage of the on-set instruction, he told the website. 'I managed to wangle a lot of training . . . I made sure that I gave the impression that I was up for it.' He explained that, aside from taking some extra boxing lessons, it was a new learning experience: 'I got free running training with the stunt guys . . . knife work and how to kill somebody in thirty seconds.' He finished with a laugh, 'kidding about the last bit'.

The film's fight sequences featured a lot of elaborate martial arts-based choreography and Theo admitted this was also something fresh for him. 'I don't really have that background, so it was kind of working with what I had . . . but I'm not nimble when it comes to high kicks and stuff.' He finished, 'It was trying to hone my own natural skill set with what they wanted.' This was Theo's first real action role and he was excited to be doing all his own stunts. 'I was up for doing as much as I could, just for the fun of it really, and to make it as real as possible.'

Theo's other main physical struggle was trying to act while wearing his vampire teeth. He told the Assignment X website that the key was practice makes perfect: 'You need to do that, otherwise you'll be lisping.' Sillier aspects of the role aside, it was a great part for Theo. He brings out an intense charisma to David's character, and with his startling blue contact lenses and naturally handsome features he delivers a very compelling performance that gives his character a genuine, animalistic magnetism.

Theo's key scenes in the film involve an extended car chase sequence through Vancouver's busy streets – although the film's insurance meant he wasn't allowed to do any stunt driving – and a couple of elaborate fight scenes, one involving the use of an extremely lethal, metal whip. Fortunately for Theo, this was a computer-generated effect, added after the movie was shot. In a long line of new experiences, this was also Theo's first time working with 'green screen' – a visual effects term that necessitates filming against blank backgrounds in order to add in computer-generated elements at a later date – and to add to this complication, the film was being shot in 3D, with two directors! Theo told Upcoming-movies.com, 'It was cool . . . I've never worked with guys who do that in a team of two, but it worked quite well, because they're so linked . . . they've known each other for a long, long time; everything they do is very intuitive.' The 3D aspect was particularly challenging as neither of the directors had worked in that format before, and were reliant on their more experienced cameraman and, in some cases, pure luck.

The shoot was a long and complicated one. With many scenes, such as the car chase sequence, the crew were forced to work through the night, often in terrible weather. Theo recalled, 'The most difficult thing was the rain in Vancouver . . . it did feel quite cold after a while.' It was a welcome relief for both cast and crew when the production moved, for a three-week period, to an indoor set, which represented the vampire coven's underground lair.

The shoot lasted three and a half months, but Theo was not scheduled to be in Canada for the entire time. The film's producer, Richard Wright, explained in the film's DVD extras, 'David had a smaller role in the film, but they liked Theo so much that they brought him back for the finale – [initially] he was not in the [final] garage scene at all.' This, despite the fact that Theo's character had actually died at the forty-eight-minute mark of the film! Thank goodness for the healing power of vampire blood. The directors joked they 'really, really hated' Theo, cursing him for being 'a perfect human being', stating, 'We killed Theo because he's perfect.' Theo had obviously made a very strong impression on the filmmakers and producers; by asking him back they had given him an enormous seal of approval and said in the film's commentary track that they felt Theo and his character definitely had potential to return in future episodes of the *Underworld* series.

Theo certainly had a lot of fun on set. He had the opportunity to spend time with Charles Dance (*Alien 3*, *Game of Thrones*), Stephen Rea (*The Crying Game*, *Interview with the Vampire*) and, of course, Kate Beckinsale. In an interview on the DVD bonus features, he describes working with her as particularly enjoyable, saying, 'It's very cool to have a fellow Brit. So we're making lots of s*** jokes together.' Again, Theo was showing he understood the need for comic relief on a hectic film shoot and he was proving to be a great asset to have on any set – always up for a challenge, but keen to keep the atmosphere lively. Perhaps it's the fact that he's a little older and came to acting late that he keeps a calm and professional demeanour, gets the work done and maintains a sense of humour while he's at it. It's a quality that makes him stand out from many of his more serious or egotistical contemporaries.

The film is far from perfect – budget restraints meant some of the visual effects shots were a little rough and ready – but it is a fun and enjoyable addition to the franchise. And, importantly, it acted as a massive stepping-stone for Theo. The look and dynamics of the character are not a million miles away from those of Tobias Eaton, and must have hinted at what he was capable of to the *Divergent* production team during their long and frustrating search to find their Dauntless leader.

During the press tour that supported the release of *Underworld: Awakening*, Theo had the chance to attend his first San Diego Comic-Con to speak about the film, and also do a bit of promotion for *Bedlam*, which was belatedly being show on BBC America. He described the event as, 'quite crazy', to the Assignment X website, adding, 'It was quite an experience. The good thing about Comic-Con is everyone's so up for it and keen that you get a really positive vibe from the audience.' As the new boy in town, the response to Theo's appearance on the panel was enthusiastic, if a little muted. He was realistic about the reception, saying, 'I'm a kind of new commodity, so it wasn't like people were screaming their heads off. But it was just nice to have good questions and positive feedback.' It is safe to assume that no one in the predominantly fan-boy Comic-Con audience was remotely interested in Mr Kemal Pamuk or the goings on at *Downton Abbey*; that in itself must have been a welcome change.

Theo attended the Los Angeles Premiere of *Underworld: Awakening* at Grauman's Chinese Theatre in Los Angeles on 19 January 2012. His date for the evening was the former *Primeval* actress, Ruth Kearney. Theo had met Ruth while they were both studying at the Bristol Old Vic Theatre back in 2009. Theo is extremely protective of his private life and has kept tight-lipped about his romantic encounters and relationships in the press, but it is rumoured they had been dating for some time. He has always insisted that he's had a long-term girlfriend during the entire period he has been in the public eye, leaving his 'young, free and single' days long behind him. He told *Cosmopolitan* in February 2013, 'I've had a girlfriend for a long time, so I don't really feel like that much of a player now. There were times when I'd go out and have some fun, but I wouldn't say I was a "playa".' He may not be a 'playa', but he was certainly turning heads in all the right places and more and more offers would be coming his way. *Underworld* gave him a taste of a bigger world.

In an ironic twist of fate, *Underworld: Awakening* was released in the US in the same week as the much delayed *Red Tails* (which Theo had completed in 2009), and it may have come as a small consolation when *Underworld* hit the number-one box office position with a first weekend gross of over $25 million against *Red Tails'* tally of just over $18 million.

But as Theo was becoming more well known and his film career was starting to take off (as well as his heartthrob status in the US thanks to the on-going 'Cult of Pamuk'), he seemed to be interviewed and photographed for fashion spreads and style magazines more than he was discussing his acting in movie and entertainment titles. Theo started to realize a lot of attention was focused on how he looked and it appears he began to feel uncomfortable with the idea of becoming a pin-up, worried that he was being seen as a model-turned-actor rather than as the trained actor he actually was. He admitted to the *Toronto Star*, 'I'm not going to pretend that I'm unhappy about getting all these fantastic jobs, but sometimes it bugs me when people want to interview me about my so-called "hotness"'. He continued, 'No one wants to be judged exclusively on that, but you have to accept it's the nature of the industry. It's inevitable.' He was quick to admit he was lucky his Mediterranean ancestry had given him certain advantages. 'Looking or sounding or being a certain way is just your genetic disposition . . . you can't shed what you are.' In the end, he acknowledged the harsh reality of the business he was in: 'I know I often get a job because of how I look, [but] I hope that I keep the job because of how I act.'

To balance out the more superficial aspects of his press coverage, Theo decided he would use the platform he'd been given to talk about more important issues such as carbon footprints and preserving the environment. He told Yahoo! Movies, 'I try to use public transport always', before launching into an attack on the half-hearted efforts that most companies make to 'go green', saying, 'They do try and make an effort, but there is a lot of plastic packaging and forks and paper cups . . . My obsession is plastic packaging; it makes me sick, all the waste. Everything about it disappoints me.' It wouldn't be too long before he would be able to share his views with a certain, similarly eco-minded, co-star on the set of *Divergent*.

After the arduous *Underworld* shoot, Theo was glad to be heading back to the UK, where he committed to a much smaller television role. The relative lack of responsibility and an easier schedule must have come as a welcome relief. It was time to start concentrating on some serious acting again.

Theo took the part of Aidan Harper in the ITV drama *Case Sensitive*. The series was based on the crime novels of Sophie Hannah and starred Olivia Williams and Darren Boyd. Each double episode centred around the unlikely working (and sometimes romantic) relationship of two police detectives as they solved a baffling murder case – this one was based on Hannah's book, *The Other Half Lives*. Theo's character, Aidan, is a talented pianist who has a dark secret in his past. He has abandoned a promising career, haunted by the belief that his actions led to the death of his controlling stepmother. He later discovers it was actually his obsessive, psychotic stepsister who murdered her own mother to free Aidan from abuse. Theo gets the chance to showcase some real acting chops as the troubled young man tortured by his own mistaken guilt and the consequences of his sister's actions. Theo would also get to show off his piano playing – or, at least, his ability to fake piano playing – in several scenes.

Case Sensitive was a fairly low-key return to UK television, but it was a solid performance that showed another side to his talents as he tries to embody a romantic, introverted but tormented musical protégé. An interesting choice, considering he had already headlined a UK television series and a major Hollywood film, but it was a clear indication of Theo's state of mind. Whether it was a conscious decision to step away from the limelight or was in reaction to feeling uncomfortable with the way he seemed to be increasingly typecast as an actor, it was during this period of relative calm that his love of music and singing would also begin to reassert itself.

Theo has stated in many interviews that he has been a member of several bands since he was a teenager. His longest musical commitment began after his time at the Bristol Old Vic. Theo had moved to London in 2010, shortly after graduating, and hooked up with guitarist Will Earl. The pair had been friends for years and had played together in several bands back home. They decided that they had enough spare time between Theo's auditions and acting jobs to put together a new band and see how far they could take it. They joined forces with a couple of Will's oldest friends and former jamming partners, Joj Sharratt on bass and Sam Sweeney on drums, and came up with the name Shere Khan. (The name comes from the tiger that features in two of Rudyard Kipling's *Jungle Book* stories, and translates as Tiger King in several ancient languages.) The band would get together whenever possible and found that they immediately clicked. Their plan of action was simple – they wanted to have fun and play the kind of music they wanted to listen to themselves.

Each member of the band brought something different to the table and this democratic melting pot resulted in some extremely productive early jamming and writing sessions. Their influences and inspirations were wide and varied and their epic and dynamic sound has obvious links to the likes of Biffy Clyro and Muse, while the underlying funkiness and groove of early Red Hot Chilli Peppers can also be heard in many of their tracks. Throw in some slide guitar and bluesy harmonica and the band's live sound starts to take shape. They had energy and drive, but they also had an ear for a good tune, giving their more melodic songs an air of Snow Patrol, Keane or Coldplay. Theo's main contribution would be his surprisingly soulful vocals and, of course, his obvious charisma as a front man.

The band announced their first official gig at The Underbelly in Hoxton Square, London on 13 March 2010. For the rest of the year, the band could be found gigging around London, slowly building a fairly small but fanatical following. They were constantly writing new songs and recording home demos. They finally got their chance to record a proper six-track demo in a recording studio in September 2010. Things were looking up. They managed to keep a steady momentum and seemed to be getting noticed. In the middle of March 2011, the band made an announcement via Facebook that they would be taking some time off from gigging due to Theo being 'away in Canada for a bit'. The truth was that this was the period of time Theo was on location filming *Underworld: Awakening*, and the complicated and extended shooting schedule meant he wouldn't be back in the UK for several months.

On his return, it was business as usual for Shere Khan. The other members of the band had been working on basic tracks and they discussed their writing methods, no doubt complicated by Theo's busy schedule, with *M* magazine. 'It varies from song to song, but often we'll share ideas via email . . . add layers before trying things out in the rehearsal studio.' It was then that the whole band would work on the tracks together to perfect the overall sound. The boys were keen to talk about further developments in their music. 'We're embracing a more layered sound on the most recent stuff we're producing, which is liberating – we've previously tried to keep things stripped back when recording.' The extra layer that was appearing in their newer tracks was a more rock–dance-orientated rhythm track, drawing comparisons to the likes of The Foals and Friendly Fires.

When asked who would be their ideal collaborator, it was clear they had ambitions to be taken seriously. 'It would be great to work with a really good producer like Paul Epworth or Jim Abbiss, who always seems to get the best out of the bands they work with,' they told *M*. They had no interest in working with flash-in-the-pan pop stars or wannabes; they wanted the men who had helped guide the careers of Adele, Florence and the Machine, Plan B, Editors and Arctic Monkeys.

By the middle of December 2011, the band were excited to announce they would be getting their first play on BBC Radio London via Gary Crowley's evening show, and by March 2012 they were definitely getting some traction at radio and picking up some buzz from record labels. In particular, the song 'Distance' was looking like the kind of track that gets a band its first record deal. But Theo's extended absence during the *Underworld* shoot was obviously not going to be his last and made organizing the band's schedule increasingly difficult. He was starting to really get noticed as an actor and offers were coming in thick and fast. The final nail in the band's coffin came when Theo was offered the lead role in US crime drama, *Golden Boy*. With the majority of the series being filmed on location in New York, Theo would have to move to America.

The band posted on their Facebook page on 22 November 2012: 'Unfortunately we are no longer actively playing together as Shere Khan. Thank you to each and every one of you for your amazing support; we had a lot of fun writing and playing our music for you. We're continuing to work on other musical endeavours, so stay tuned and watch this space! – Much Love – Will, Theo, Joj and Sam.'

In another life, it's easy to speculate that Theo and Shere Khan might have enjoyed greater success in the music industry – a charismatic lead singer is sometimes all it takes to get a band started on the road to international success and a long and creative career. Inevitably, Theo would have to choose between his two possible professions and it was becoming clear that Theo had been well and truly bitten by the acting bug. The lead role in a promising and intriguing new US drama, as well as the chance to temporarily relocate to New York, was too good an opportunity to miss.

Golden Boy was conceived by two US television veterans, Nicholas Wootton and Greg Berlanti. Wootton had worked his way through the ranks as a writer/producer on series such as *NYPD Blue*, *Law and Order*, *Chuck* and *Prison Break*, while Berlanti had been a writer and producer on several high profile series including *Dawson's Creek*, *Brothers & Sisters* and *Everwood* – which he also created. In recent years, Berlanti's success rate has gone through the roof: in the same season that he launched *Golden Boy* with CBS, he also had his biggest success to date as creator of *Arrow*, the ratings-busting superhero drama airing on the CW Network in the US and Sky 1 in the UK.

When asked to compare the two shows and explain what would make *Golden Boy* stand out from the many other cop shows airing at that time, Berlanti told *The New York Times*, 'You're not dealing with someone putting arrows in people, so it's less dark. But you're dealing with human emotions, and in a way that makes it darker.' Wootton, who has extensive experience writing in the crime genre, was also keen to stress the show had a unique edge and was conceived as a slight twist on the tradition, saying, 'This is a show about a character who can make mistakes, but you still forgive him for those mistakes.'

The show would ask difficult moral questions such as 'What is the true price of success?' and 'How far will you go and how much are you willing to sacrifice to reach your goals?', as well as exploring the ugly, destructive force of ambition. It was obvious it was going to take a lead actor with a lot of raw charisma and genuine emotional complexity to portray its main character, Walter Clark. The whole series would focus on Clark, charting his meteoric rise from New York beat cop to Chief of Police in an unprecedented period of time. The majority of the story would be told in the present day, detailing Walter's career progression from naïve cop to police detective, with each episode bookended by a 'flash-forward' of seven years to see Walter in his role as Police Commissioner. In these scenes we would see the mental and physical toll this rapid climb to power has taken on Walter.

As with most network television shows in the US, the main cast attached to *Golden Boy* would be expected to sign a standard contract that would see them committed to the project for the next seven years. The ultimate aim for Berlanti and Wootton would be an ongoing, seven-season story arc, each season covering a year in the progressing career of Walter Clark. The series would have a slowly unravelling mystery at its centre, as we find out the truth about Walter and what he has had to do to get to the top. Slowly, each season would move towards closing the gap between the present day and the flash-forward sections.

In early February 2012, it was announced CBS would be making the pilot – at that point untitled – and Ryan Phillippe would star as Walter Clark. It would appear that while Phillippe was attached everyone had grown uncomfortable with the title *Golden Boy*, perhaps worried it misrepresented the darker, more complex subject matter of the show or that it might recall the 'blonde pretty-boy' tag Phillippe had been desperately trying to escape for most of his career.

Phillippe had risen to celebrity in the late 1990s in such films as *I Know What You Did Last Summer*, *Cruel Intentions* and *54*, before really hitting the headlines as the husband (and ultimately, ex-husband) of Reese Witherspoon. Despite critically acclaimed performances in *Crash* and *The Way of the Gun*, he had struggled to maintain a lasting profile on film and had turned to television. He had taken guest roles on several shows, including a multi-episode arc on hit legal drama *Damages*, but this would be Phillippe's first time as the lead in a television series since his debut acting job, almost twenty years previously, in US daytime soap *One Life To Live*. Within weeks, however, it was reported that Phillippe had grown nervous about committing to the intense production schedule of a potentially long-running network television series and had amicably withdrawn from the project. The producers were left high and dry, with the full supporting cast in place and only a matter of weeks before filming was due to begin on location in New York. With Phillippe gone, the title *Golden Boy* was reinstated and Berlanti and Wootton set about frantically looking for another actor to play the lead role of Walter Clark.

Phillippe's sudden and unexpected departure seemed to inject the production with a new energy and everyone involved was determined to get the show back on track, and more importantly, on air for the proposed February 2013 launch date. The urgency involved in finding a replacement meant the producers were unable to see every actor in person, so they were holding auditions via video as well as setting up face-to-face meetings. As luck would have it, Theo was between jobs when he heard about the role in *Golden Boy* and was able to audition from his base in the UK. He told *The New York Times*, 'Not that long ago you had to be in LA . . . now you can send a tape from London and it arrives in fifteen minutes.' Impressed with what they saw, Berlanti and Wootton quickly offered Theo the job and he was on his way to New York within a few weeks.

When Philadelphia radio station 98.1 WOGL asked Theo why he thought more and more English actors were playing Americans on television and in films, he joked, 'I think it's because we work for [basic pay]. We're a lot cheaper.' This would be a pivotal moment in Theo's career, exposing him to life-changing career opportunities and experiences that would stay with him forever.

Theo had been to America once before, but in very different circumstances. Just eighteen years old, before he started university, he had travelled around the US by bus on a very tight budget. He told *Bello* magazine a story about taking his first bus trip to LA. 'There was this big, overweight woman in a grey sweatpant suit, and she kept staring at me, and she was like, "What? What?!" And then she just started pissing herself . . . the whole time saying "What's your problem?"' He concluded with a laugh, 'So that was my first impression.'

The opportunity to start living and working in New York City was a dream come true for Theo. Taking to it like a duck to water, feeling very much at home and acting like a native in no time, Theo told *Glamour* magazine, 'One of the books I read for research said that [locals] can always tell a tourist because they are always looking up at the skyscrapers. After that I never look up – "I'm not a tourist, I'm a tough guy!"' he teased. He was immediately struck by the vibrancy of the city and couldn't help but compare it to London: 'The difference between New York and London is that things are boring and staid in London. But even the sh***y diners and bars here are kind of exciting to me.' He continued, 'Everywhere you look there is something happening.'

He was beginning to feel at home and was hitting the town to take in everything the city had to offer. 'It feels very safe to me. People say that New Yorkers aren't friendly, but I think they're more friendly than Londoners ... You can go out on a night out and meet ten random people and stay in touch with them, whereas that's not going to happen in the same way in London.' He told *Bello*, 'I loved it ... I'm kind of obsessed with it. I love the culture and the vibe and iconicity of it and the island of Manhattan being so small and filled with that kind of hyper-exuberance that you don't get anywhere else.'

Just being in the city and understanding its rhythms was going to be important in understanding the basics of his character, Walter, and the character of the show itself, he revealed to *Glamour*. 'It plays such a big part in the series. I think you can tell when a New York show isn't shot in the city. It's so iconic and has such a specific energy.' He went on to explain its value, 'For me, it's extremely useful because it means it's another weapon in my arsenal to being as deeply seeded in the character as I can be ... Also, it's fun! It's one of the greatest cities in the world.'

Unfortunately for Theo, there wouldn't be too much down time. He was now under a great deal of pressure to get up to speed with the rest of the cast and join a production that was set up and ready to go. With very little time to prepare for the role, he would have to undertake an avalanche of research. This included reading 'on the job' autobiographies such as *Blue Blood* by Edward Conlon – Conlon was a former police officer who regularly wrote for *The New York Times*, and his memoir lifted the lid on the unglamorous reality of police work, from cop brutality to the aftermath of 9/11 – and hard-hitting cop novel, *Clockers*, written by Richard Price, a senior writer on ground-breaking television series *The Wire*, as well as binge watching television series such as *The Shield*. Theo explained his main research was spending time in the city of New York itself, hanging out with native New Yorkers and being allowed to go on 'ride-alongs' with active police officers. He was lucky enough to spend time with an experienced homicide detective, allowing him to sit in on real interviews and interrogations. This direct research would prove invaluable, Theo told *The New York Times*: 'New York cops are very specific in terms of the way they talk and the way they handle themselves.' It would be perfecting that swagger and recreating the cop attitude he had initially assumed was nothing more than cliché that would be key to finding the basis for his character. 'I thought [they] were from a bygone era or were a bit of poetic license with cop shows – the more you hang out with them, the more you realize how real that jargon is.'

He also had a very short time to perfect an authentic New York accent. He told *Cosmopolitan* that the key to maintaining his accent was making sure he never let it slip. He said, 'I think [*Homeland*'s] Damien Lewis said this, but I just basically had to speak in the accent from the moment I got in the van to go to the set 'til the weekend'. He shed more light on his method on Philadelphia's 98.1 WOGL radio station, saying, 'The best way to do it is to speak with the accent all the time – you want it in a place where it's so natural that you never have to think about [it], because if you're thinking about the accent, you're not thinking about the scene.'

The show had a permanent advisor, an ex-cop with years of service on the streets and as a 'cold-case' detective, who would help Theo with other detailed research such as the broader aspects of the law, tactics and correct working practices – including arrest procedure, booking criminals and interview technique. He was also given extensive training on how to convincingly handle and fire a handgun. He even spent a few evenings drinking in cop bars, telling *Glamour* magazine, 'That's when the really meaty stuff comes out – when people can talk a bit more freely.' He went on to say he'd developed a newfound respect for the work New York cops do. 'It does genuinely seem unlike any other in America and, even, the world . . . There's a very specific cultural dynamic, a specific chemistry. There's almost a specific set of rules because of the city and the size of it.'

The final key ingredient would be creating believable relationships between the characters on the show. Spending time with the advisor, Theo realized very early on that cops who work together form very strong bonds, and their shared experiences means there is a heightened understanding between them. He expounded this bond to *Glamour* magazine: 'Our advisor's ex-colleagues are his family. You spend so much time with them and share so much because you see a lot of s***, a lot of death, and a lot of pain. Inevitably, you're going to become close to each other.'

Theo's main co-star would be Chi McBride, whose character, Detective Don Owen, acts as a mentor and father figure to Walter. McBride is a seasoned US television veteran, having appeared in shows as diverse as *The Fresh Prince of Bel Air*, *Pushing Daises*, *House* and *Human Target*. Their on-screen chemistry would be at the heart of Walter's ultimate redemption and a vital ingredient in the success of the show. In an interview with *The New York Times*, Theo explained the importance of the relationship to his character's journey. 'In the beginning, he is definitely a lone wolf. He's very closed, very single minded. His relationship with Chi McBride's character opens him up. It becomes a father–son thing, and he begins to respect other people and take advice, which he didn't before because he was such an arrogant b******.'

Talking to the *Pittsburgh Post-Gazette*, Theo discussed the relationship further, saying, 'They're teaching each other, and Chi's character is the old guy who's kind of given up, and I'm bringing out the best in him. And then with me, he's tempering my central morality between whether I choose the darker nature that Clark leans towards . . . or I use the law for the purpose of good.' Theo was aware of a parallel with their situation in real life, he said to the Deadline website, 'It's a little bit of art imitating life,' he explained. 'I'm a young English punk coming over, and McBride is a veteran actor. So there was a lot that we could learn from each other, and we had a good natural chemistry.'

McBride himself was keen to point out, in an article published by the *Huffington Post*, that 'Cop dramas are pretty much as old as television itself . . . but the difference is that this is more about relationships than just the "case of the week".' The pair bonded very quickly and formed a credible and appealing double-act that helped drive the show's central premise.

With the meat and bones of his character in place, Theo had to create a convincing psychological profile for Walter Clark. Theo revealed his initial attraction to the character was based on two things: he was keen to tell the story of one ambitious man's rise to power, exposing the ruthlessness required along the way, while also exploring the delicate balance of loss and gain that accompanies success. He explained to *The New York Times* that he was also drawn to the opportunity to show the duality of Walter, a man who, early in his career, has sacrificed his personal life and his fundamental beliefs to take a high profile job in public office. 'I get this great chance to play two differing personalities. You have this young, naïve, cocksure guy who's kind of willing to do anything to get what he wants, and then you flash forward to a man who feels older than his age.' He went on to reveal that during the research period, when on patrol with real police officers, someone had said, 'Aren't you a bit young to be a cop?', reassuring Theo that this displayed 'good symmetry with the story'.

The show's creator, Greg Berlanti, told the *Los Angeles Times* it was this mix of youth and ambition, exemplified by real-life characters such as Facebook founder Mark Zuckerberg, that was key to the show's relevance. 'We're at a moment in our culture where we see young people have a lot of aspirations and success that I'm not sure they're always ready for . . . And there's very good drama in whether they're going to sink or swim.'

The world Walter moves in is brutal and corrupt; he is dealing with some extremely dangerous people and entering into shady deals for his own advancement, and most of the time we see he is completely out of his depth. Theo had already experienced the scary world of the supernatural in *Bedlam* and *Underworld: Awakening* and he was keen to explore the fear which exists in more true-to-life situations, he told the Assignment X website. 'Power and politics and someone screwing you over and jailing you for fifteen years when you didn't do anything wrong – that's also extremely scary.' Although Theo would describe Walter as 'a bit of a player' to *Cosmopolitan*, he admitted there was a lot more to the character; it was the complicated inner journey that would be the most interesting element of his development during the first season of the show. 'He's also a bit of a loner and he protects himself emotionally, but he ends up meeting [a woman] and he kind of opens up to her and starts maybe showing a bit of his vulnerable side.'

The pilot episode opens with a dramatic shoot-out between

the twenty-seven-year-old Walter, his partner and a couple of armed robbers. Walter's partner is shot and left for dead before Walter manages to take down both of the criminals and then, miraculously, bring his partner back to life using CPR. It is this act of heroism that launches Walter on his rapid upwards trajectory.

Given his choice of promotions, he chooses to become a New York City detective. It's not long before there is a jump forward in time of seven years and we see Walter at age thirty-four, taking up office as Police Commissioner and quoting advice from a former mentor. Theo cuts a very impressive figure in these opening scenes, believably wide-eyed as the rookie cop, but also suitably charismatic and weather-beaten as the older, wiser Walter.

As the episode returns to the present day, we meet the other detectives working out of the 39th Precinct. Detective Christian Arroyo is Walter's role model and it's obvious he idolizes him from their first meeting. Walter assumes he will be partnered with him but is hugely disappointed when he is introduced to Detecive Owen – his actual partner. Owen is African-American, overweight and a twenty-three-year veteran of the job, a far cry from the cop Walter pictures himself becoming. Detective Deb McKenzie is the only female detective in the squad and she is partnered with Arroyo.

Over the course of the action, we see Walter is a very intuitive detective, but his displays of tentative bravado and ever-present cockiness are soon exposed as a front for his insecurities and inexperience – paper covering the cracks his instant promotion has created. As the episode plays out we meet Walter's vulnerable, possible drug-addict sister and we witness a more compassionate side as he tries to keep her out of harm's way.

Theo gets to show off a lot of his developing acting skills in his first forty-five minutes of primetime drama: aside from a very credible New York accent and his impressive handling of the many action set pieces, we see him, as Walter, coming to terms with the reality of his situation. Betrayal and disappointment are written all over his face during the closing scenes where he realizes, far from being his potential mentor and role model, Arroyo is in fact a corrupt and manipulative negative force within the squad. As a result, Walter finally accepts Owen as the true guiding light for his career and it is then Owen delivers the speech Walter was seen quoting in the opening flash-forward sequence: 'Twenty-three years on the job, been exposed to a lot of human nature, a lot of surprises. But one thing always holds true: inside every man, there's two dogs fighting. One's good, one's evil. You know who wins? The one you feed the most. And the sooner you get rid of this pit-bull pride of yours, the sooner you'll be teachable.'

The very last scene is a flash-forward that cleverly sets up the season's main story arc and lays out several intriguing questions, teasing that the story has a lot of secrets to reveal before the seven-year gap between Walter's past and present is closed.

A promising start, the pilot episode aired on 16 February 2013 with substantial, if not headline-grabbing, ratings. It reached over 10.5 million viewers and the critical response was largely positive. Dorothy Rabinowitz of the *Wall Street Journal* said the show 'is packed with fine performances', while Verne Gay said in *Newsday*, 'The best stuff in *Golden Boy* is the little stuff – sharp, brittle dialogue, nice performances and street cred that's a cut above average.' Alan Sepinwall of HitFix.com said the series was 'a solid, meat-and-potatoes police procedural, and one that could potentially evolve into more, depending on how the flash-forwards are used down the road.' *Daily News* agreed the characters were

Although Theo rarely mentions his love life in the press, he has been rumoured to have been seeing fellow actor Ruth Kearney, with whom he is pictured here at the *Underworld: Awakening* premiere *(above)* and taking a stroll through New York, 2012 *(right)*.

(Facing Page) Shailene takes home what is surely to be one of many gongs to come as she collects the 2012 Independent Spirit Award for Best Supporting Female for her role as Alex King in *The Descendants*.

(Above) Shailene, also, does not spill much about her love life, as she is pictured here with ex-boyfriend and *Secret Life* co-star Daren Kagasoff at *The Descendants* LA premiere.

(Right) Honestly, not a crush: Shailene and George Clooney attend the Annual Directors Guild of America Awards in Hollywood, 2012.

(Above; below left) Theo demonstrates another aspect of his talents in 2012's *Case Sensitive*. (Below right) Shailene meets *Divergent* author Veronica Roth after she is announced as Tris Prior in 2012. It wouldn't be until Spring 2013 that Theo would be cast as Four.

(Top) Jumping for joy: Shailene had great fun working on *The Spectacular Now* with co-stars (l–r) Brie Larson and Miles Teller and director James Ponsoldt.

(Left) She shows just how far she has come as she calmly answers press questions at a screening of the film in Summer 2013; (above) not so calm as she dances at the after party with Miles Teller.

The Golden Boy: Theo looks the part as cop Walter Clark, alongside Chi McBride *(above)*, in 2013's *Golden Boy*, and relaxing on set with Bonnie Somerville and Kevin Alejandro *(below)*.

(Above) Eventually united as Tris and Four, Shailene and Theo share a joke on the *Divergent* panel at San Diego Comic-Con 2013.

(Below) Shailene showcases her shortened locks, courtesy of her part in *The Fault In Our Stars*, while presenting an award at the 2013 Gotham Independent Film Awards.

One film will transform them: bright futures lie ahead for these two young stars, and we can expect them to be Divergent together for some time to come.

strong – 'We quickly care what happens to these characters, which gets any show off to a strong start' – but questioned the time-jump framing device, saying, '[it] makes the story feel more complicated than it needs to. *Golden Boy* doesn't need to be framed as a series of implicit or explicit flashbacks to engage us as an adventure tale.'

Some critics were not so kind, with a few particularly unwilling to buy into the time-swapping device. Mary McNamara, in her *Los Angeles Times* review, described the show as 'an ambitious character-driven drama over-enamoured from the get-go with its tricky structure and coy premise', before concluding, '[it's] a shame. CBS does have its share of highly successful, fairly workmanlike procedurals, but it also has *The Good Wife*, which created the template for stories that balance rich character and compelling plot. *Golden Boy* could have done that as well. But it doesn't.'

McNamara's attack was not reserved exclusively for the show; she also had her claws out for Theo, saying, '[Theo] spends most of the pilot looking intensely at the floor just behind the camera in order to offer us a three-quarter profile that someone, apparently, thinks exudes Strong Emotion.' In response to the links the show's producers had made to Mark Zuckerberg and *The Social Network*, she delivered another right hook, hammering home her point: 'there is something of Jesse Eisenberg's shark-eyed blankness in James' performance, but the passive aggressiveness of a college geek simply doesn't work for a cop. And with those cheekbones and that chin, James too often appears to be posing for a Calvin Klein ad.' Harsh words indeed, but they do illustrate a problem Theo had been facing more and more: was he being taken seriously as an actor?

The initial promotion for the launch of the series involved

selling Theo to the American audience as a major new heartthrob and this included erecting a giant billboard in Times Square featuring a shirtless picture of Theo. While he was quick to make light of the poster in a radio interview with WOGL 98.1 – 'That's in my contract: must show butt' – he realized there was a more serious issue to address. He told the *Toronto Star* he didn't know whether to laugh or cry, joking, 'I didn't study classical theatre at the Bristol Old Vic so that something like that would happen.' Theo began to appreciate his time as a relative unknown, who was used to blending into the background, would soon be over.

He had mixed feelings about the use of sex to sell the show, telling *Cosmopolitan*, 'It's always a bit of a wrestle . . . nudity is a part of life. You don't mind doing it as long as it furthers the story. But when it doesn't, that's when you need to question it.' In the interview with the *Toronto Star* he reasoned that hopefully it would be his acting and the depth of his research that would shine through. 'You need to trust your instincts . . . you just pray when the moment comes you can slip inside the character, otherwise you're just that bloke with no shirt on, looking stupid up there on some giant billboard. And I don't want that to be me. No way.'

In *Golden Boy*, the network had a buzzy, stylish drama along the same lines as ABC's *Revenge* or *Scandal*, one that could attract a similarly youthful audience, as well as appealing to the slightly older, more sophisticated viewer who was tuning in to watch *Homeland* or *The Good Wife*. Instead, marketing that featured Theo as television's latest hunk seemed to be aimed more at fans of *The Vampire Diaries* or to follow the 'hot-guys-in-uniforms-and-tight-tee-shirts' route employed on recent hit fireman drama, *Chicago Fire*. Viewers tuning in to see Theo in romantic clinches or caught off-guard in 'just-out-the-shower' shoot-outs were sorely disappointed by the confusing marketing strategy CBS had used to launch the series. It had pulled them in with the promise of some eye candy, but the show failed to deliver, with Theo remaining fully clothed throughout the pilot episode.

Such a strategy to sell a police procedural featuring ambitious narrative devices clearly didn't accurately reflect the series's content, and may have gone some way to explain why reviewers such as McNamara took issue with how the show was presented. Indeed, hers was a fair representation of the opinion shared by many critics and viewers who had tuned in to see the first episode, challenging how *Golden Boy* was misrepresented as well as the story itself.

Golden Boy was not reaching the audience that would fully appreciate the intricate storylines and equally complex characters. Ratings started to slip, and the show lost about one million viewers per week before averaging out at around 7 million for the rest of its run, the same number that tuned in for the season finale in May 2013.

The show was 'in the bubble' – a term US television executives use to describe a series that is standing on the knife-edge between being renewed for another season and cancellation. With shows existing on the borderline of renewal, many factors can come into play; low ratings do not always result in cancellation. A low-rated show with a highly engaged fan-base can avoid the cut, while a modest ratings success can find itself on the scrap heap if the budget versus income equation doesn't add up. It usually boils down to a simple question of mathematics and money: Is the show too expensive to produce? What is the return on every dollar spent? Where can we cut the budget?

It would appear there were two things that would seal *Golden*

Boy's fate. The show was an unusual twist on a tried and tested genre and expected its viewers to commit to a slow-reveal story arc. Most successful dramas on television follow the same blueprint of a self-contained story told within each single episode. Any network series that challenges that formula – *24*, *Lost* or, more recently, *Revolution* – has to come out of the traps with a bang, grab big ratings and keep building the mystery or drip-feed the answers all the way to the series finale. *Golden Boy*'s ratings were average. It was obvious the central premise of the show wasn't enough of a hook for the audience and the show's viewing figures were only likely to go one way. This, coupled with the fact that the show was primarily filmed on location in New York rather than on the back lot of a studio, made it considerably more expensive to produce than most mainstream network shows.

During this time of uncertainty, the search for an actor to fill the still vacant leading male role in the film adaptation of *Divergent* was reaching fever pitch. The hunt for Tobias 'Four' Eaton had been a long and frustrating one for director Neil Burger and the team at Summit Entertainment. They had auditioned, or at least spoken to, hundreds of young actors. Many of the more high-profile names mentioned in leaks to the press or suggested online in 'fingers-crossed' Twitter messages had not proved to be right for Four. But there was one young actor who had caught the eye of the *Divergent* team. They were convinced that Theo was the one they had been looking for and expressed interest in casting him. The only problem being that he was still contracted to an ongoing television series.

It's hard to say if the uncertain future of *Golden Boy* was the final hurdle the *Divergent* producers had to cross to get the man they wanted – maybe they would have hired him regardless – or whether Theo's enthusiasm to be cast as the film's male lead was the last nail in *Golden Boy*'s coffin, swinging the balance from renewal to cancellation. Whatever went on behind closed doors between CBS, Theo, Burger and Summit entertainment, an official announcement was made on the 10 May 2013 that *Golden Boy* had been cancelled, with the *Hollywood Reporter* stating, 'During its freshman run [the show] averaged 8.3 million viewers – solid, but not the breakout critical hit the network had hoped for.' So, after much negotiation, the show's demise meant Theo was now completely free to commit to Tobias Eaton and *Divergent*. The only questions remaining were: Was he truly Dauntless and brave enough to take on another Hollywood franchise? Did he really have what it takes to become Four?

Chapter Seven

SHAILENE: A SPECTACULAR FUTURE

As Jennifer Lawrence was being photographed on the red carpet at the LA premiere of *The Hunger Games* in March 2012, it had been over eighteen months since Shailene had starred in anything high profile, outside of her commitment to *The Secret Life of the American Teenager*. It was reported she had turned down several major film roles, including the title character in the remake of horror classic *Carrie*, a part that eventually went to Chloë Moretz. Shailene seemed to have decided juggling jobs and playing the 'Hollywood game' was too stressful. Constantly losing out to other actresses was frustrating and she took the time to concentrate on enjoying herself and exploring her other interests. She explained her thought process to the *Los Angeles Times*: 'I don't want to play the game of cat and mouse, where I have to do this part so I can get that part', and revealed her long-term views about acting as a career, saying, 'if it's meant to be, it's meant to be. If not, I'll be a third-grade teacher'.

By removing herself – however temporarily – from the movie

treadmill and the politics of Hollywood she'd always disliked and tried to avoid, Shailene had managed to rekindle her love of acting. Her desire to make interesting movies with edgier characters was still very much alive. In the six months following the release of *The Descendants*, Shailene's next two film projects were announced. She would play Aimee Finecky in *The Spectacular Now* and Kat in *White Bird in a Blizzard*. Both of these films would be independent movies – made outside the Hollywood system – and both projects would be completed either during breaks from her *Secret Life* schedule or after she was released from her contract.

On reflection, Shailene was adamant that awards and acclaim, although appreciated, were not the reasons she'd got into film acting – they were elements of the industry she felt removed from. She told the *Hollywood Reporter*, 'I'm an artist; I'm not a celebrity, or famous, or a star, and I never, ever, ever will be, because that's not my goal.' Shailene felt the position she now occupied would allow her to deliver an important message. She wanted to use that platform to educate and inform. 'What I'm really excited about – and it took me a long time to get it, to understand it – is that I have the ability to spread love and compassion back into the world. That's why I'm here.' The things that interested her as an adolescent – nature, education and health – had become something she was now intensely passionate about. It's easy to conclude Shailene's time in Hawaii was more than just a professional high-point and speculate that she had also experienced a personal awakening that would allow her to fully ignite some long-held passions and ideas.

Shailene's personal philosophy regarding the environment is fairly simple – it has to start with how you treat your own body. She believes it is extremely important to educate oneself about the food we eat so we are aware of the chemicals we put into our bodies. Only when we take control of our own health and practise an environmentally responsible and non-impactful lifestyle can we look outwards and, as a vital part of the eco-system of the planet, try to improve things on a worldwide scale.

Growing up, her parents were aware of the basics of healthy living, but did not enforce strict rules about eating healthily. She told *Coco Eco* (an environmentally aware magazine that promotes sustainable eating, fashion and beauty), 'I was raised in a family that said, "We're not going to eat white bread, but we'll eat wheat bread", but of course that still has artificial colours and flavours.' Having been raised in Simi Valley, she knew how precious and fragile the balance of nature could be. She was taught to respect it and understand the need to preserve it.

Shailene's personal mission to educate people about the environment was born when she was a teenager in high school. She was struck by the everyday pollution she saw in her own schoolyard, with leaves blowing in the wind and mingling with the trash from lunchtime recess. She found herself more and more involved with environmental groups, reading books on the subject and volunteering.

Shailene explained that her real epiphany came when she read a book called *Farm Sanctuary* by leading animal rights activist Gene Baur. In the book, Baur sets out to examine the impact of eating meat on humans and animals. It raises ethical questions about factory farming, meat production methods and how, as individuals, we can live better lives and educate others by stopping the mistreatment of animals and promoting compassion towards others. Shailene saw how this could run parallel with many of her own views.

Her grandmother was a naturopath and a big influence on

her future lifestyle. She believed in alternative medicine and non-invasive treatments – avoiding surgery and modern 'bio-medicines' – using natural remedies and promoting healthy eating and a healthy standard of living. When Shailene was fourteen years old, her grandmother had tested her blood and told her the results had suggested she should eat more vegetables and that using microwaves was a bad idea. Shailene instantly started her own research and she began to alter her diet – she also says she's never used a microwave again since that day. Shailene started by eating more vegetables and cutting down on processed foods. She also started foraging for food as a hobby, teaching herself the nutritional value or medicinal qualities contained in certain wild plants and vegetables growing locally. She doesn't eat anything made using genetically modified products and states that although she is not a vegetarian or vegan, she only eats meat that has been humanely raised. 'I would rather actually kill my meat than buy it in a plastic wrap.' She continued to *BlackBook* magazine, admitting her views were fairly extreme, 'If I eat meat, it's organic, but beyond organic – only twenty chickens on a farm instead of nine hundred. And I actually go to the farmers and order directly from them.'

She started to volunteer at a family owned organic farm called Vital Zuman in Malibu, a few miles south of Simi Valley. She would go there whenever she had days off, or needed to unwind. She explained to *Malibu* magazine, 'They have a farm stand. I go, and they tell me what they need done, and I farm. And in exchange, I get free vegetables.' She collects her own natural spring water and takes it everywhere she goes. When away from home filming or promoting projects, she always takes her own packed lunch, rather than rely on others meeting her dietary needs.

Keen to prove that her theories of 'pay-it-forward'-style education and 'every-little-helps'-encouragement do work, she told a story about her uncle, who owns a large food production and catering service. He had been fairly dismissive of Shailene's attempts to educate him about organic foods, sustainability and the impact one company can have on the environment, saying he felt the whole organic movement was a fad which would quickly die out. But over time, Shailene illustrated the harmful impact of some of the processed foods he was using, stressing he had a responsibility to provide better quality, more environmentally safe products for his customers. Eventually, she was able to persuade him to change some of the company practices. 'He didn't know anything, and was using plastic forks and plates, but now he has shifted into eco-friendly compostable ware for the food, and although most of the food is still not organic, the meats are and he is trying to source from local farms.' She concluded, 'It inspires me to see the baby steps people take, but the lack of information is really frightening.'

Aside from health and environmental issues, Shailene feels very strongly about using the platform she has been given to highlight other problems she believes need addressing, whether they be political struggles or social injustices such as sweatshops or the rise of Monsanto, the world's largest developer of genetically modified crops.

Shailene has said on several occasions that she is not interested in celebrity, or the fake empowerment it brings. She told the *Chicago Tribune* that the real dirty words in Hollywood are not swear words. 'The F-word is "famous", the C-word is "celebrity" and the S-word is "star",' she said, continuing, 'famous, celebrity and star, I think, are misused. Unless you're George Clooney and can't go to a baseball game without being smothered, you're not allowed to use those words [to describe yourself].' Conscious the film and television industries present a very specific picture of what beauty is, she has also spoken out against the use of photoshopping in magazines and advertising, aware it can be seen as harmful if it is promoting an unhealthy and unobtainable body image to girls her age. Shailene has never been 'super-skinny' and has always seemed completely comfortable in her own body.

She has firm views on Hollywood's fascination with fame and the materialism it encourages, taking issue with people in the public eye using their positions to endorse products she considers unethical or unhealthy. She built on this while talking to Collider. com, 'Nothing really attracts me to this industry . . . I look at acting as an art, and that's all it is for me . . . the reason I keep doing it is that it fuels some sort of passion in me, but the day that those butterflies stop is the day that I'm gonna quit because I could care less about the magazine or being famous or the money or the awards.'

Shailene may have been spotted at a few 'Fashion Week' events, but she has never really been interested in high fashion. She told *Coco Eco*, 'I'm very lucky to work with a stylist who cares about fashion, because I don't at all.' She states she is much more interested in buying used or vintage clothes. She promotes recycling and the 'up-cycling' of clothes, spending hours looking for bargains in thrift shops or at trade-in and second-hand clothes stores. She's not against having a rummage through her friend's closets either!

Initially, Shailene struggled at red carpet events, feeling she was being hypocritical by publicising a certain designer or showing off a dress she would only wear once. She came to a perfect compromise, however. 'Obviously, I'm going to wear a dress to go to [an awards show]; I'm going to be respectful. But I'm not going to let my life revolve around it,' she continued to *Coco Eco*. She resolved to only endorse clothes she could wear and then donate to charity or recycle – she would make it clear in interviews that this was her intention. 'I think it's a great message to send. I do wear those fancy dresses and suits, but I am not keeping them. I wear them and then return, then someone else wears and returns, and so on, and it's this beautiful re-use and restore process.'

Shailene's other charity work initially came as a by-product of her connection to *Secret Life*. As an unofficial spokeswoman for the show, she was quick to point out that the series dealt with real problems – such as sexual health and unwanted pregnancy – but delivered them as entertainment, with dramatic license. She had read a number books in preparation for the role and felt she should try to educate people and promote responsible attitudes towards sex, the importance of sexual health and the harsh reality of teenage pregnancy whenever possible. This led her to volunteering and undertaking charity work for the Children's Foundation and the Elizabeth Glaser Pediatric AIDS Foundation, among others.

By the summer of 2012, as her scheduled August hiatus from *Secret Life* loomed, there was no let up for Shailene as she prepared enthusiastically for her next film role as Aimee Finecky in *The Spectacular Now*. Ensuring she was beginning a trend that started with *The Descendants*, this would be the second of an extended run of book to movie adaptations that would dominate her choices and continue with *Divergent* and *The Fault In Our Stars*.

The Spectacular Now is based on Tim Tharp's young adult novel about coming-of-age and would be directed by James Ponsoldt. Talking to *Entertainment Weekly*, Ponsoldt described the script, which brought him on board, as 'lovely, emotional, powerful and, for me, it was the most honest depiction of adolescence that I've ever read.'

He had received plenty of critical acclaim for his last film, indie drama *Smashed*. That film, about an alcoholic couple – played by Mary Elizabeth Winstead and *Breaking Bad* star Aaron Paul – dealt with the consequences of trying to stay together while only one of the pair strives to get sober. It picked up the Dramatic Special Jury Prize for Excellence in Independent Film Producing at the Sundance Film Festival in 2012 and renowned film critic Roger Ebert gave it 3.5 stars out of 4, describing the film as, 'a serious movie about drinking, but not a depressing one.'

It was no surprise Ponsoldt was attracted to *The Spectacular Now*. The novel tells the story of Sutter Keely, a popular high school 'party-boy' who is dumped by his girlfriend when she refuses to deal with his borderline alcoholic antics. He is befriended by Aimee Finecky, a shy loner – the kind of girl who isn't really popular at school, but isn't an outcast either. She is bright and quietly ambitious, self-contained and bookish, but is held back by her controlling mother and her social awkwardness. Aimee and Sutter begin a tentative and unconventional relationship. As the story unfolds, Sutter realizes that through the choices he makes, he has the power to change both of their lives forever. Sutter struggles to make the necessary compromises and, as the story comes to an end, we are left wondering if Aimee can save him or if he will continue on his own path of self-destruction.

Shailene had kept a distant, watchful eye on the development of the project for over two years. She had made it known she was interested in playing the female lead from the moment she read the script, penned by the writers of *(500) Days of Summer*, and she was determined not to let this one slip through her fingers. Ponsoldt had said of the story while talking to EW.com, 'This is exactly what it's like when teenagers fall in love for the first time, and have your heart broken', so it is no wonder that this theme had also struck a chord with Shailene – hardly a stretch for the girl who'd been playing teen mom Amy Juergens for the last four years. But Aimee Finecky was a completely different character. It was clear Shailene went out of her way to avoid the high school drama and the social rollercoaster Amy Juergens filled her life with. Ponsoldt describes Finecky as 'a little socially awkward, but she's so much more profoundly mature and soulful' – not the naïve, but ultimately empowered young woman Amy Juergens had become.

With the role secured, Shailene sat down with her director to discuss what sort of picture they had both imagined making. It turned out they had similar ideas. They wanted to make something truthful and meaningful, avoiding the multiple clichés of most teen movies. Shailene told EW.com that they would aim for 'a [contemporary] movie that has the feel of a John Hughes film'. Like Hughes's movies *The Breakfast Club* and *Pretty In Pink*, Ponsoldt wanted his movie to have an element of fun, to explore some of the scary excitement of first-time adventure and the dizzy optimism of youthful hopes and dreams, as well as having the sense of silliness that accompanies the angst of growing up. It also had to have something more serious going on under the surface – an exploration of the deeper, more uncomfortable feelings that real adolescents all experience but don't want to admit to.

Although the part was originally offered to Nicholas Hoult

(*About a Boy*, *Warm Bodies*, *X-Men: First Class*), Shailene's co-star, in the role of Sutter Keely, would be Miles Teller. Teller had made a startling debut in *Rabbit Hole*, playing opposite Nicole Kidman and Aaron Eckhart in a role that won him a Best Supporting Actor nomination at the Chlotrudis Society for Independent Film Awards. He had also appeared in the stage version of *Footloose*, which led him to reprise the role in the 2011 film remake, and had recently carved out a niche for himself playing out-of-control college students in films such as *Project X* and *21 & Over*. In his *Entertainment Weekly* review for *The Spectacular Now*, Owen Gleiberman said, 'Remember how Elvis Presley looked when he was young? Imagine Elvis reincarnated as a tall and brainy American high school dude, with a quip for every occasion, and you'll have an idea of the fresh yet slightly skewed charisma of Miles Teller.' The credibility of his performance is central to the success of the film and he manages to maintain the perfect balance between a cocky, wisecracking, but always charming character akin to Matthew Broderick in *Ferris Bueller's Day Off*, and the more rebel-without-a-cause angsty figures of River Phoenix or a young Johnny Depp.

Shailene said to EW.com, 'Everybody should have Miles Teller on their film' and described him as 'such a gentleman', which is just as well, because this film took Shailene into some potentially uncomfortable, uncharted territory – her first sex scene. *Secret Life* had infamously 'talked the talk' as far as sex was concerned and it had obviously dealt with the consequences of it, but being a family oriented soap opera, it had stayed very much on the coy side of scenes of a sexual nature. In an interview with her *Descendants* co-star Judy Greer in *The Lab* magazine, Shailene revealed that she wasn't afraid of nudity, and that she was very comfortable in her own skin and had previously enjoyed the freedom of being naked on a nudist beach on her travels through Italy. 'It's so refreshing to be around people who don't attach a stigma to sexuality,' she said. Similarly, she has described her passion for nude photography, explaining, 'I think there's something powerful about being a human and being strong in a state of vulnerability where you have no clothes on . . . I think it's beautiful and I like to apply that to my art . . . I do get a lot of inspiration from that.'

Ultimately, she knew she was in the hands of a respectful director whose only agenda was to portray something raw and intimate. She could relax and trust that nothing appearing on screen would be gratuitous and would only service the story. In the end, Shailene described this scene as her favourite in the whole movie. 'We wanted it to feel real and private. So many times [a movie version] of losing your virginity is glamorous. That's just not the case in real life,' she said to EW.com. By the end of filming, Shailene would say of Ponsoldt, 'I'd do anything and everything for him.'

The film was given a limited release in August 2013. *Entertainment Weekly* gave the film an A– score, saying that it was 'one of the rare truly soulful and authentic teen movies. [It has a] rich and exploratory psychological texture, but it's not afraid of being an all-out teen movie.' The *Washington Post* praised the film for its realism: 'With its quiet moments and easy pace, it effortlessly illustrates the realities of being a teenager, with the awkward first times and the casual selfishness, the drive to rebel but also the need to feel loved.' It went on to say, 'So often, we go to the movies to escape real life, but the wistful *The Spectacular Now* proves that revisiting reality can be so much more powerful than avoiding it. The movie captures the raw excitement and heartbreak of adolescence so completely that it manages to replace a seen-it-all jaded heart with the butterflies that accompany fresh experiences.' The *San Francisco Chronicle* described the film as 'original, truthful and moving', before pointing out that 'the key is that it's not about the phenomenon of being young, but rather about the particular characters', concluding, 'it's not that anything especially astounding happens, but rather that the typical things don't – and the things that do happen are things that might happen in real life.'

Other reviewers were quick to focus on the two young leads. Movies.com said their performances were 'solidifying Miles Teller and Shailene Woodley as future movie stars', while the *Chicago Tribune* said, 'Woodley is genuinely wonderful in it. And Teller's right behind her.' In one of the last reviews he wrote before his death, esteemed film critic Roger Ebert said, 'What an affecting film this is. It respects its characters and doesn't use them for its own shabby purposes. How deeply we care about them.'

Initially playing on only four screens in New York and Los Angeles, the film took a healthy $200,000 in its opening weekend. Following strong word of mouth and a positive critical response, *The Spectacular Now* expanded through late summer and is estimated to have grossed in the region of $7 million in the US. The film played as part of the London Film Festival ahead of a UK release in early 2014. In late November, as speculation began about who would be the big winners in the upcoming awards season, it was announced Shailene had been nominated by the Gotham Independent Film Awards in the Best Actress category for her performance in the movie. Unfortunately, this time she was unsuccessful, but here's to hoping this season will bring the first of many honours for the role.

On 9 October 2012, shortly after Shailene finished filming

The Spectacular Now and returned to work in LA, ABC Family announced that the fifth season of *The Secret Life of the American Teenager* would be its last. Falling ratings meant the network had no option but to cancel the show. Creator Brenda Hampton summed up her feelings about the end of an era in an interview with EW.com. 'It was like a second family . . . We spent so much time together . . . I loved going to work every day. And though the job presented a lot of challenges, I'd have to say that [*Secret Life*] was also the best job of my life . . . the years went by so quickly!'

An ambitious and restless Shailene probably didn't share that sentiment exactly, and her feelings were undoubtedly not quite so clear-cut. While she was obviously extremely proud she'd been part of such a groundbreaking show, she must also have felt an enormous amount of relief. Unquestionably glad she'd stayed true to her original reasons for taking the role and still filled with overwhelming affection for Amy and her *Secret Life* family, she would have been excited about the possibilities that were now opening up for her. She told Moviefone.com of the mixed blessings she'd experienced as part of a long-running series. 'I think doing anything in life you learn things. And the biggest learning lesson from that was actually paying attention to what you do. Because when you do sign a contract, you do sign [away] a portion of your life . . . you make a commitment. And you stick to that commitment.' With only the final twelve episodes left to complete and another three months left on her contract, Shailene was finally able to take full control of her own destiny. But with typical down-to-earth charm, she bid a fond farewell to the show that had become such a huge part of her life and broadened her horizons as an actress, saying, 'I'm so glad [that I did] the show, oh my gosh, it's been such a fun ride.'

Shailene was now free. She had some big decisions to make about her future. Was her dream of taking time out to study still alive, or was she now more determined than ever to pursue a full-time career as a film actress? It seems like the decision was quickly made for her. A mere twenty-four hours after the *Secret Life* cancellation announcement, EW.com reported Shailene had been offered the role of Mary Jane Watson in the upcoming *The Amazing Spider-Man* sequel. The internet chatter had barely calmed on that story when a week later the news leaked that Shailene was in talks to star as the lead in another potential movie franchise, *Divergent*.

When Shailene was first offered the part of Beatrice 'Tris' Prior, she wasn't sure it was the right move for her at that point in her career. She had always said she wanted to connect with characters and stories on an emotional level, to see the reality in what was written in the script. In an interview with *ASOS* magazine, she said, 'I'd rather, at this point, do a small scene in a Meryl Streep movie than do the lead of a superhero action movie. I really respond to human scripts, scripts that are raw, and real, and risky.' She told EW.com about conversations she'd had with people she trusted; they warned her, 'If this thing turns out to be a *Twilight* or a *Hunger Games*, this or that might happen.' Only just coming out of her five-year run on *Secret Life*, she was obviously wary of making another long-term commitment to a single project. She was enjoying her newfound creative freedom and was worried where the *Divergent* juggernaut might take her. 'After [*Secret Life*] I never want to sign a contract for more than a year again.' She continued, 'My agents were like, "Are you f****** crazy?" But I said, if this movie is successful, things will change and I don't know if I want that.'

In the end, she said 'Yes', and her journey into a very different world began. Perhaps she took some inspiration from one of her favourite actresses, Natalie Portman. Shailene had already spoken of her wish to work with filmmakers like Darren Aronofsky, specifically mentioning *Black Swan* as an example of the dark and complex movies she aspired to make, but it must be remembered that before *Black Swan* bagged Portman her Oscar in 2011, she had played Queen Amidala in the *Star Wars* prequels trilogy and was currently two movies into her stint as Jane Foster in Marvel's ongoing *Thor* saga.

Before she wasted another moment asking herself 'What would Natalie Portman do?', there was the small matter of filming her next movie. Shailene was used to a hectic working timetable, but 2013 was shaping up to be her busiest yet. She had committed herself to filming three projects back-to-back, a schedule that would see her on set for almost six months straight. At the end of it she would have another indie drama and two blockbuster franchises to add to her CV.

First up was *White Bird in a Blizzard*, an adaptation of a French novel by Laura Kasischke. Shailene would play Katrina 'Kat' Connors, a seventeen-year-old girl whose life is turned upside down by the disappearance of her mother, the mystery that is revealed during her search to find her and the after-effects the answers have on her life and the people around her. The film would be directed by Gregg Araki, a fiercely independent American filmmaker whose insistence on portraying the dark underbelly of American society has meant he has consistently failed to get US funding for his projects, leading him to seek financing from European sources. His previous films have explored sexual abuse, eating disorders and teen depression, but he is best known for the movies *The Living End* and *Mysterious Skin*. The latter starred

Joseph Gordon-Levitt, an actor whom Shailene had previously mentioned as an inspiration, which may explain, in part, her attraction to *White Bird*.

The cast featured some well-known faces, including Eva Green (*Casino Royale*) as Eve, Kat's beautiful yet enigmatic mother, Christopher Meloni (*Law & Order: Special Victims Unit*) as her father, Brock, Shiloh Fernandez (*Evil Dead*) and Mark Indelicato (*Ugly Betty*). Araki told Screenslam.com, '[the film is] similar to a movie like *American Beauty*', describing the thriller as 'tense and dysfunctional'.

Set in the late 1980s and early 1990s, the film has a dark, almost gothic tone. Shailene also talked about the project to Screenslam. com, outlining its broad appeal: 'I think a lot of people who are older will be able to look back on their adolescent era and relate to the "goth" aspect of it, or the dreariness or the angstiness, and teenagers who exist today will be able to relate to the feeling of not ever being enough, or not ever being able to freely express themselves.' Shailene described her character Kat as 'kind of your typical angsty teenager when you first meet her ... then as the movie progresses you find out there was a lot of turmoil and underground tribulations that nobody knows about.' She concluded, 'It's very relatable ... a lot of families feel this pressure to be something that they are not and it ends up creating a lot of inner destruction because you're not allowed to freely express your emotions and feelings and you end up stifled in that way.'

The project was completed in a matter of weeks. Although it was thought the film would play at the Cannes Film Festival in 2013, it did not appear on the schedule and is still awaiting a release date in the US. It's almost certain Shailene and the film will be doing the rounds on the 2014 indie festival circuit, as it seems more than likely the film will surface in the wake of one of her more high-profile projects.

Shailene's next stop would be another film set, in another city. She was off to New York to complete her scenes for *The Amazing Spider-Man 2*. After the first movie had made over $750 million at the global box office, it was no surprise a sequel was green-lit almost immediately. The film had received mixed reviews and was considered a fairly underwhelming addition to the already over-populated superhero genre, but director Marc Webb was determined to up the ante on his hero by piling on the pressure in the sequel, with bigger and better villains and an increase in the emotional stakes with extra portions of romance and teen dilemma.

Shailene would be playing Mary Jane Watson, a character who had been introduced in the comic book series as a rival to Peter Parker's steady girlfriend, Gwen Stacy. Mary Jane (played by Kirsten Dunst) had featured as Spider-Man's main love interest in Sam Raimi's original trilogy, yet her character did not feature in the 2012 re-boot at all – Andrew Garfield's Spider-Man had Gwen Stacy as his main squeeze, as played by Emma Stone. The sequel, much to internet fan-boys' excitement, obviously planned to stir up some romantic rivalry between the web-slinger's two most famous girlfriends.

As well as the returning Garfield and Stone, the cast was rounded out with the additions of Dane DeHaan (*Chronicle*) as Harry Osborn, Chris Cooper as his father Norman Osborn and Jamie Foxx and Paul Giamatti (*Sideways*) playing super-villains Electro and the Rhino respectively.

Filming began in early February 2013, with several pictures of Shailene on location in New York being leaked in the press and online. In them, Shailene sported her newly dyed chestnut hair, a pair of tight, ripped jeans and a cool black jacket. She was pictured filming scenes with Emma Stone and Andrew Garfield. Her time on the set was short – just three days – as she went straight from New York to prepare for her next job as Tris Prior in *Divergent*. It must have come as a huge blow to Shailene when, in June 2013, Marc Webb announced her scenes were being cut from *The Amazing Spider-Man* sequel and the character of Mary Jane would now appear in the third film, scheduled to be released some time in 2016. Shailene told EW.com, 'Of course I'm bummed', before continuing, 'but I am a firm believer in everything happening for a specific reason. MJ only appeared in a few scenes and I wouldn't trade the experience of working with Andrew and Emma for three days on set for the world.' She graciously concluded, 'Based on the proposed plot, I completely understand the need for holding off on introducing MJ until the next film.' Fingers crossed, then, that we see MJ facing off against Tris Prior in an *Insurgent* (the *Divergent* sequel) versus *Amazing Spider-Man 3* showdown at the box office sometime in 2016.

However, that is still a little way in the future, as there was still the small matter of filming the first *Divergent* movie and making sure it lived up to the success it obviously had the potential to be. With Shailene, and a hugely talented supporting cast on board, that was looking like a sure thing. Shailene travelled to Chicago to begin preparation for filming, but as the rest of the cast gathered to join her and start training, one important character was conspicuous by his absence. It wasn't until mid-March that year that the studio announced they'd found their male lead: Theo James would be joining the cast as Tobias 'Four' Eaton.

Chapter Eight

THEO: BECOMING FOUR

THE SEARCH TO FIND THE PERFECT ACTOR to play Tobias 'Four' Eaton had been a long and exhausting one. In the book, Four is described as over six foot tall with a solid muscular build. He has short hair, as befits his faction, and deep-set, dark blue eyes with long lashes. He is eighteen years old, two years older than Tris, who finds him frustratingly aloof and somewhat distant during their first encounters. He is stern and serious, as if weighed down by the burden of his responsibilities and obligations. Slowly, as he and Tris begin to spend more time together, his attitude starts to thaw and their mutual attraction gives way to something more intense and intimate.

To be convincing as a Dauntless leader, the actor playing Four necessarily had to be strong and athletic. Although the book never describes Four as being particularly attractive, in the transfer to the big screen, him also being handsome would obviously work in the film's favour commercially. Eye colour aside, Theo seemed to be the perfect fit as far as the physical aspects of the character were concerned. But to be truly accepted in the role he would need to deliver something more than just a strong and masculine performance; he also needed to be credible in his more vulnerable and quieter moments.

The first problem that casting needed to address was the fact that Tris, in the book, is supposed to be sixteen on 'choosing day' and Tobias eighteen when the two first meet. However, Shailene would actually be twenty-one when *Divergent* started shooting. Age was less of a worry for her – on camera she looks young for her years and was well versed in playing younger characters – yet the relative age of Four was still an issue. It was unlikely any eighteen-year-old actor was going to be able to display the required gravitas as Four when standing beside Shailene. The decision was made that they would hire an actor who was slightly older. This is hardly without precedent in Hollywood – Olivia Newton-John and John Travolta were actually twenty-nine and twenty-three respectively when they were playing 'teenage' high school sweethearts Sandy and Danny in *Grease*. In the same film, Rizzo was played by thirty-three-year-old Stockard Channing. And far from being a 'Baby', Jennifer Grey was actually twenty-six when she played schoolgirl Frances Houseman in *Dirty Dancing*.

The call went out towards the end of 2012 for actors in their early to mid-twenties. There was no shortage of eligible candidates – Hollywood was bursting at the seams with good-looking, talented young actors and the producers appeared to be spoilt for choice. As always, these early casting sessions and auditions were shrouded in mystery and the first round of meetings were held behind closed doors, far from the prying eyes of the *Divergent* fan base. The first actor to break this silence and announce via Twitter, rather prematurely as it turned out, that he had an 'amazing' meeting about playing Four was Alexander Ludwig. He was well known to *Hunger Games* fans as Cato, the brutal and ruthless Tribute from District Two. Yet, more names were to appear.

Within days, the floodgates were open and rumours and wild speculation began – speculation that would not stop until the eventual casting of Four some five months later. Along the way, Colton Haynes was reported to have quit his lead role on the hit MTV show *Teen Wolf* to be able to join the cast of *Divergent*. As it turned out, an offer to join ABC's hit superhero series, *Arrow*, was more tempting. It seems clear that the producers' initial thoughts were to cast a relative unknown to play Four. As the months went by, the casting rumours continued. Front runners seemed to be Luke Bracey, a former *Home and Away* actor who had appeared in *G.I. Joe: Retaliation*; Brenton Thwaites, another former *Home and Away* actor; Lucas Till, who has a recurring role as Havok in the *X-Men: First Class* series; and Jack Reynor, an American who was relatively new to acting but received much critical acclaim after being cast in Irish drama *What Richard Did* while studying in Dublin. All these actors were rumoured to have 'chemistry tested' with Shailene, but still no announcement was made. *Entertainment Weekly* added its own favourite picks to the list, putting forward Dane DeHaan – who was riding high from cult science fiction movie *Chronicle* and would soon be announced as taking on the role of Harry Osbourne in *The Amazing Spider-Man* sequel – Nicholas Hoult, who had just finished filming *Warm Bodies*, and Jake Abel, who had come to prominence as Luke in the *Percy Jackson* series and would soon be playing Ian in the film adaptation of Stephenie Meyer's post-*Twilight* novel, *The Host*.

Then the news broke that two more high-profile actors had entered the race. Jeremy Irvine's star was certainly on the rise. His first film was Steven Spielberg's *War Horse*, quickly followed by lead roles in *Great Expectations* and *Now Is Good*. It is rumoured he was also offered, and subsequently turned down, the role of Peeta Mellark in *The Hunger Games*. Many believe he was Neil Burger's first choice to play Four. At the same time, another actor with previous young adult credentials was also moving to the top of Burger's list: Alex Pettyfer. The English-born actor had been heralded as 'the next big thing' on two separate occasions. His first brush with fame came in 2006 when he was only fifteen, cast as would-be spy Alex Rider in *Stormbreaker*, the first in a proposed series of films based on Anthony Horowitz's extremely popular Rider novels. Unfortunately, it failed in the US and was considered a huge critical and financial flop. Alex's next big break came in 2011 when he was cast in the screen adaptation of the coincidentally named young adult science fiction novel, *I Am Number Four*. Although it wasn't a financial failure on the scale of *Stormbreaker* – the film recouped its $50 million budget at the US box office – plans for a proposed sequel were quickly abandoned. Ultimately, neither Irvine nor Pettyfer were right for the role.

Around this time, Shailene decided to rally the troops. Maybe she was growing impatient waiting to find out who was going to be 'her' Four, as she told MTV, 'The thing about Four is that he has to be a man. No feminine actors, please.' She went on to offer some fairly pointed 'friendly' advice to anyone who intended to audition. 'You need to not have muscles that [just] look good and [don't] actually work . . . It's a natural masculine power that some people have and some people don't . . . This character needs to be extremely masculine, and his eyes need to scream vulnerability and sensitivity. It's hard to find in a dude, especially a dude who can act.'

By mid-March 2013, with filming due to start in less than a month, the race to cast Four was entering the home straight. The names at the top of the list were beginning to thin out. It is rumoured Jeremy Irvine was offered the role but declined – he feared being typecast as a romantic lead and held broader ambitions as an actor. He has since committed himself to a wide range of smaller projects including the sequel to Daniel Radcliffe's *The Woman in Black*. Alexander Ludwig also tweeted he had recorded another screen test – it was obvious a decision was imminent and a name would shortly be announced. What nobody expected was for that name to be Theo James.

Veronica Roth told the BrodartVibe review website that she'd grown more fond of the character of Four the more she wrote about him, saying, despite the book being told completely from Tris's point of view, 'I felt he had a life beyond what Tris observed, with a history she was able to discover as the book went on. Even when he wasn't around Tris, I felt like I knew what he was doing, so he was very real to me.' She also told the Novel Novice website that she wasn't interested in casting celebrities when it came to *Divergent*. 'I love to see unknown faces in movies, and see what people make of someone I've created in my own head. I'm open to anyone who brings something to the character.' A tall order, she and Summit Entertainment were about to put their money where their mouths were by casting someone with a relatively unproven box office record as the male lead, in what they hoped would be the next major Hollywood franchise.

There are no advance reports of Theo's auditions or screen test. We can only assume that, as a relative unknown, he was off the radar for most of the casting process. It could also be he had been ruled out fairly early on due to his standing commitment to *Golden Boy*.

Theo had maintained a passing interest in the role of Four, but he had learned the best thing to do in Hollywood was to stay level-headed and avoid getting your heart broken. It's safe to assume that watching the bright and beautiful in Hollywood jockeying to fill Four's shoes that he had subconsciously removed himself from the race, concentrating instead on his full-time job as the lead actor in *Golden Boy*. As ratings fell, CBS had been on the fence about cancelling the series – if they decided to renew the show for another year, Theo would be contracted to stay with it indefinitely. This was undoubtedly a predicament Shailene could relate to.

The final decision was made; the axe fell and Theo was released from his *Golden Boy* obligations. Theo had already joined the rest of the *Divergent* cast on set in Chicago when the official announcement was made a few weeks later in April – *Golden Boy* had not been renewed for a second season. Theo hit the ground running. As well as reading the script, he had immersed himself in research for the part, reading the *Divergent* and *Insurgent* novels before he turned up for filming. During an event at the San Diego Comic-Con he told the audience the first thing that hit him about Four was the fact he was not just another heartthrob; there was real depth to the character, he said. 'He's quite old school, and I think he's a man with this very centred sense of masculinity and he's not afraid to demonstrate what he's afraid of.' Theo concluded, 'I think, ironically, that makes him more masculine and tougher.'

Theo recognized his looks had inevitably played a part in his landing the job – after all, it was a big Hollywood movie and Four would definitely be seen as a romantic figure – but he was keen to underplay the 'pin-up' image that had started to dominate any discussion of his work. With Four, he had the chance to redress the balance a little and play a character who, while he was undoubtedly going to be gracing the walls of many teenage girls' bedrooms, was more three-dimensional. His personal challenge would be to make him more true to life than the likes of Jacob Black or Edward Cullen.

Eric Feig, president of production at Summit's parent company, Lionsgate, explained the long and difficult process of casting Four in a general press statement. 'We took our time to find the right actor to fill the role of Four, and Theo is definitely the perfect fit,' going on to stress that Theo was perfectly equipped to embody the beloved character from the source novel. 'Veronica has crafted a truly iconic character in Four, and we cannot wait to begin production and bring him and this story to life for millions of fans around the world.'

The success of the film would rely heavily on getting the hardcore fans of the books to buy in to the movie adaptation; only then would they be able to use that ready-made fan base to spread the word and turn the movie into a genuine blockbuster. A key factor in getting those fans on board would be their acceptance of Theo as Four. Theo told EW.com, 'As a fan of *Divergent*, I am thrilled to have been chosen for the role of Four and to be a part of such a phenomenal story.' He continued, 'Along with the incredibly talented Shailene Woodley, we are looking forward to the fantastic adventure of bringing this beloved book to life on the big screen for all the fans.' A fairly transparent attempt to get the passionate *Divergent* readers on his side, certainly, but maybe he had already seen some of the fans' initial responses to his casting, which was, to put it kindly, rather mixed. Not since the news that

Daniel Craig would be picking up his licence to kill as a blonde and much more rugged James Bond in *Casino Royale* had there been such an enormous backlash to a casting. Reactions on fan forums and comment boards attached to casting announcement features ranged from the blunt 'No' to the more unusual criticism that Theo might be 'too good looking' to play Four, many stating that in the book he is described as 'not traditionally handsome', with a hook nose and ears that stick out. One argued they were glad a 'standard heartthrob' type had not been cast and Theo's acting ability would count for more than his looks, highlighting his work in *Golden Boy* and saying, 'he brings something raw and unusual to his character'. Another fan was sure Theo was the right choice saying, 'he has the look and the hint of darkness'.

Predictably, the main stumbling block seemed to be the fact that Theo, at twenty-eight, was ten years older than Four. Many complained he would just look too old next to Shailene. Some reasoned Four's Dauntless past would have taken its toll, ageing him and making him seem older, while others simply stated it was fitting that he looked older than Tris; it would give him an air of forcefulness and authority – after all, he was supposed to be her Dauntless instructor. The film's director, Neil Burger, told the *Los Angeles Times*, 'I couldn't be happier that Theo James will be playing the role of Four. It's rare that you find someone who can do it all: he's tough and charismatic; a fighter and a lover. And he and Shailene Woodley have a remarkable chemistry – sparks truly fly between them.'

The last word on the subject would go to Veronica Roth. She had, after all, created Four and had a better understanding of what qualities he should possess, and what he should look like, than most. She told Teen.com that Theo was the only actor who had completely matched her vision for the character, and when she saw his screen test she had let out a sigh of relief, stating, 'There's a reason they cast [Theo].' When asked by the PagetoPremiere.com to describe him, she said, 'Handsome, intense, sensitive and badass.' Roth admitted she did have her own concerns about the age difference, however. 'I was most concerned about the age gap looking okay . . . I think that [in photographs, the actors] look a lot older than in real life. I'm like, "Oh! Yeah, this is not a problem" . . . [after] seeing them all together, they definitely look younger than you think.' She went on to reveal that she had always worried an actor in their late teens might struggle to portray the complexity of her characters on the big screen: 'I think that was crucial to making this movie work and by casting older actors we definitely have gotten that maturity, which is amazing.' Roth was also quick to dismiss any criticism that some of the casting did not match details of the characters as written in the books, saying, 'What I was most concerned about when they were casting was finding actors who could capture the internal world . . . as opposed to exactly matching the description.' She insisted she was more interested in hiring good actors who could bring something new to the characters she had created, declaring, 'I would be a little disappointed if it was exactly how I pictured [the characters in the books] because there's then no re-interpretation, no new discovery.'

It would be 'new discovery' all the way for Theo as he entered the world of *Divergent* and met the girl he would, potentially, be spending a lot more time with – Miss Shailene Woodley. Shailene immediately went on record, telling Hypable.com that Theo was, 'the perfect Four', before highlighting their relationship and how it had grown from a quickly established friendship and discovery of mutual interests, saying, 'we're not into "The Industry" and have separate lives outside of it. That's refreshing.' And, as if to prove their shared easy-going nature and playful attitude towards the job was already in sync, she added with a laugh, 'I don't know what I would do if Four was played by someone who cared what he looked like or spent more time in front of the mirror than I do.'

Chapter Nine

SHAILENE: BECOMING TRIS

ALTHOUGH THE CASTING OF BEATRICE 'TRIS' PRIOR would be a piece of cake in comparison to the months of searching it took to find Theo and cast him as Four, it wasn't without its obstacles. *Divergent* author Veronica Roth told journalist Ben Falk on his website, 'It's hard to cast Tris – she's not pretty, and most actresses are!', while Shailene Woodley revealed in conversation with Andrew Sims of Hypable.com, 'I never wanted to do big films. Especially one that was similar to *The Hunger Games* or *Twilight* – something with a huge fan base that would carry on for years.' These were just two very early difficulties that highlighted how it would take a bit of work to get this perfect combination of actress and character together.

In the book, Tris is described as looking young for her age, her rather plain, but not unattractive, face giving her a generally unassuming presence. She is of average height and build, has long blond, wavy hair and her piercing blue eyes are framed with a dark, almost black, outer ring. She is aware of beauty in others

– her mother, for example – but her Abnegation upbringing has conditioned her not to place a high value on physical appearance and there is definitely no place for vanity in an Abnegation household.

Roth explained the importance of casting Tris to the BrodartVibe website, saying her entry point to the entire *Divergent* universe was through its main character. 'I was pulled in by Tris. I was fascinated by her voice, and I first wanted to create the circumstances in which that voice emerged, and then see what she could tell me about what was happening in her world.' Roth knew that only by creating a well-rounded and believable heroine would she be able to keep readers involved in the science fiction elements of the story. She explained her guidelines to the Confessions of a Bookaholic blog: 'I did set myself a rule that was hard to follow . . . Beatrice is always the agent. That is, she's always choosing, always acting, always moving the plot by her behaviour.' She conceded, 'I don't know if I succeeded in keeping that rule, but it was helpful for me when trying to create an active, rather than a passive or reactive, character.' Roth admitted an important part of making Tris relatable was by giving her some of her own personality traits, telling Goodreads, 'Tris and I have a lot in common. We both feel a little awkward in social situations, we're a little too serious for our own good, we tend to be straightforward and assertive, we both feel this overwhelming need to face our own fears. She's braver than I am, but then, I'm a little more compassionate.'

It was only much later in the writing process that Roth was struck by how alike they actually were. She told one Twitter follower, 'I wrote it without realizing she was at all like me. Now I see that she has the qualities I need to face my own struggles.'

Unlike the heroines of similarly themed young adult novels,

Tris was not interested in the misery of an unrequited love affair or willing to get involved in a complicated love triangle. Roth told NovelNovice.com, 'Love triangles are great, but they're just not a Tris thing. She's just so focused on what she wants.'

The actress who would eventually play Tris had to be more than just a pretty face; there had to be something going on behind the eyes. Roth had told one Twitter follower she liked their choice of Saoirse Ronan, replying, 'as long as we're speculating, Mia Wasikowska is very close to what I imagined.' On the whole, Roth was surprised by most of the fantasy casting suggested by fans, telling MTV's Hollywood Crush blog in mid-2011, '[Fans] usually pick someone for Tris who is much more gorgeous than she is. Tris is supposed to be plain.' She stated, 'If I had a dream cast, it would be people who are relatively unknown or anyone who can capture the sort of tough but vulnerable spirit Tris has.' She concluded, 'I'd rather have a good actor than an actor who looks just right.'

The news of Shailene's casting as Beatrice 'Tris' Prior in October 2012 must have come as something of a 'hallelujah' moment for Roth, as it was for the millions of expectant *Divergent* readers, relieved the wait was over. Convinced lightning was unlikely to strike twice – they'd already had their perfect Katniss Everdeen, brought vividly to life in *The Hunger Games* movies by Jennifer Lawrence – many undoubtedly worried they'd end up with Miley Cyrus, Selena Gomez or another Disney Channel graduate in the role. Upon hearing Shailene was in talks for the part, Roth wrote in her blog, 'From the moment I heard that she was being considered, I have been nothing but enthusiastic', and, when asked about Shailene's suitability, she wholeheartedly gave her blessing, telling Hypable.com, 'Shailene brings reality. Tris is an impetuous sixteen-year-old . . . she has kind of a harsh personality, with some vulnerability. And I think all of the shades of what Tris is, is what Shailene is able to do.' She expanded on this idea, saying, 'Physically, what's important to me, more important than other aspects of her appearance, is that Tris does not look like an action hero – she looks like a slight person with youthful, delicate features, someone who shocks you with how strong and capable she becomes.' She officially gave her seal of approval by referencing Shailene's previous work: 'To me, that [Tris's] is exactly the look that Shailene has, exactly the look I've always had in mind . . . I'm confident she will be able to capture Tris's particular mixture of vulnerability and strength, and that surprising moment when a seemingly unremarkable girl from Abnegation transforms into a powerful yet flawed woman . . . I wasn't that surprised [at her casting] because I saw her in *The Descendants*.'

On the day after the news of Shailene's casting broke, EW.com ran Tara Fowler's article entitled 'Five reasons Shailene Woodley could make a great Tris in *Divergent*'. In it, Fowler made reference to the fact that Shailene had auditioned for *The Hunger Games* and therefore was 'familiar with the kind of audience *Divergent* will attract and that she's prepared to take on the responsibility of playing a character that could draw a lot of attention – media and otherwise.' She went on to praise Shailene's acting chops, citing *The Descendants* rather than *Secret Life* as the best indication of what she was capable of. Although she was quick to dismiss Shailene's work on the latter, she did point out that her time on the long-running show proved she respected her own work and had shown unwavering commitment to the role of Amy over a five-year contract. She would, without a doubt, see the *Divergent* saga through to its conclusion – anywhere up to four movies, if the producers decide on a split two-movie adaptation of *Allegiant*, the final book in the trilogy. She then turned her attention to Shailene's physical attributes, stating she had a 'young face' and looked believable as the 'scared' sixteen-year-old who turns up at the Dauntless training room in the book's early chapters. She finished off by saying, 'Woodley's not a badass, but she looks like she could be.' Joking about Googling bikini shots online to check Woodley's suitability, Fowler asked, 'Aren't you tired of too-thin girls getting these meaty action roles and tossing 400 lb men over their shoulders?' In the books, she says, 'Tris might be small, but she was strong,' and concluded that, in her opinion, Shailene looked like she fitted the bill. Fowler – and everyone else – would find out soon enough.

What really swung the decision for an initially reticent Shailene was her uncovering elements of the book directly related to her own interests, as well as the relevance of some seemingly futuristic ideas to events that are already happening in today's society. Shailene pointed out that in the book, the population is controlled by an injected serum; in real life we insert identification chips into dogs and, in some cases, even into babies. She told Hypable.com, 'After reading the book I was really profoundly moved. [The book is] very metaphorical for things that are going on today. Specifically things that I'm passionate about, and things I want to make public, and things I want to educate people on. So I think it's a really great platform.'

Getting into the mindset of Tris, a confident young woman who knows her own mind, who is willing to make difficult, life-changing decisions and appears strong enough to deal with the consequences wasn't too much of a stretch for Shailene; she'd been playing that part all of her life. Understanding the frustrations and restrictions of a faction-based society, as well as the enormously physical elements key to the role would be Shailene's biggest obstacle. She told MTV, 'I think that a big thing is just pretending that I live in that world. It's a world that's so different from today . . . thinking of [*Divergent*'s] dystopian world and living in different factions and not being allowed to express your multiple personalities. Being constricted to one thing is going to be the challenge.'

There would have to be some truly demanding combat training in order to convince anyone Tris (and ultimately, Shailene) was worthy of her place. But Shailene's take on the character, as you might imagine, was slightly different to most, as she told the San Diego Comic-Con audience. 'I never see her as a superhero or an action star. I saw her as a very normal young woman who had to figure herself out as well as help the community around her . . . put in very elevated situations, she's forced to find herself through those experiences and I thought that was really neat and a rare opportunity.'

Shailene had recognized that Tris, while more feisty than your average teenager, was relatable to many girls her age, musing, 'I think all of us are extremely brave and extremely courageous but I don't think that we're necessarily put in situations where we're forced to call upon our bravery.' She understood teenagers faced tough choices in their real lives and hoped Tris would inspire them to find their own inner strength. 'What I loved about Tris is that she was in the situation and she rose to the occasion and found the bravery within her to help those around her as well as help herself.'

Rising to the occasion was something that came naturally to Shailene; she had overcome some fairly serious personal issues in her time and faced some frustrating and taxing professional challenges. Like Tris in the book, she wouldn't have to face everything alone. She had her very own Four, in the shape of Theo James, and they were about to enter the *Divergent* world together.

Chapter Ten

SHAILENE AND THEO: CREATING TRIS AND FOUR

AUTHOR VERONICA ROTH DESCRIBED her writing process to the Goodreads website: 'Wake up. Blink a lot. Eat breakfast. Drink tea. Attempt to start writing. Get distracted. Take a shower. Get dressed. Attempt to start writing. Get distracted. Eat lunch. Attempt to start writing. Actually start writing! Write until five. Get exhausted. Stop writing.' Amidst so much procrastination, it's a miracle she has managed to finish one *Divergent* novel, let alone three!

Veronica Roth was born on 19 August 1988. She wrote the majority of *Divergent*, her first novel, while she was still in her final year of a three-year writing course at Northwestern University in Illinois. The course involved spending each of the three years studying one specific category – creative non-fiction, poetry and fiction – before choosing a preferred topic. She found she was more suited to the fiction writing class and ultimately this would become her passion. In fact, this process doesn't sound too dissimilar to the journey taken by her most popular creation, Tris Prior. In the world of *Divergent*, she too would discover her own aptitudes and then undertake extensive training to become an accepted member of her newly chosen faction. It is these choices and their consequences that dominate Roth's books, and her understanding of them makes her particularly suited to writing within the young adult genre.

Roth has said her interest in young adult fiction, and in particular dystopian-themed young adult fiction, stems from her own experiences at high school. The genre echoed her mindset and the intensity of emotions she felt at the time, and reflects the important choices the majority of young people feel they have to make during that period. She could still relate to that confusion and told Robin Young in an interview on the *Here & Now* radio show, 'I don't know very many people who remember high school with total fondness . . . there's a reason for that!' She continued, 'When I was sixteen, I really did feel like I had to choose the rest of my life because everyone was putting a lot of pressure on all of us to figure out where we wanted to go to school next or what we wanted to do if we weren't going to school . . . I really didn't feel like I knew myself all that well. It seemed natural to me to reflect that experience in these books.'

Roth wanted to explore and understand the stresses involved in trying to define yourself as an individual and the fear you will never be allowed to make your own choices in life. She explained to the *Wall Street Journal*, 'These books have main characters that take charge of the world that they're in, whether it's fair or not. Most of them are in relatively powerless positions but they find [a purpose] and act.' She finished, 'This is an idea that is really resonant in teenagers, for obvious reasons.' She built on this while talking to the Confessions of a Bookaholic blog, suggesting 'dystopian books are perfect for people who like to ask "What if?" but want to see their "What if?" questions played out in a world that has the same rules as our own – as opposed to paranormal or fantasy, in which the rules of the world [might be] a little different.' She concluded, 'There is something extremely interesting about looking at the world now, reading about a possible future world, and imagining the steps in between.'

The idea of writing books for young adults has always been Roth's goal, and she cites Roald Dahl as an early inspiration, simply 'because he's awesome', she told the YAHighway.com, admiring his ability to tell stories that were 'funny, dark and touching all at the same time'. She has also spoken on several occasions about her love for the Harry Potter books, revealing to *USA Today* that '[J.K. Rowling's] attention to detail and world building is definitely something to aspire to. The world of Harry Potter is so intricate.' Like Rowling and Dahl, she wanted her readers to identify with the characters she had created more than anything else. To her, that was far more important than where they lived or what adventures they took part in. Even if they were boy wizards or ended up visiting an imaginary chocolate factory, the reader would feel connected enough to the characters to let themselves become fully immersed in the story, wherever it took them, in whatever form. She told the BrodartVibe website, 'I have found that most of the characters that fascinate me are under eighteen. There is something compelling about that age. You are old enough to make your own decisions, but not experienced that you know what to choose. Every struggle feels like life or death because you're forming who you are.'

Much later, when *Divergent* had been published and Roth had started promoting it via book tours and meeting young readers, her choice was validated, she told the Best I've Read blog. 'They asked the most insightful questions . . . it confirmed for me that I was writing in the right genre for me. And I realized that having readers, especially ones who care that much about the characters and their stories, makes writing far more gratifying.'

The final touches to the *Divergent* world would also benefit from her love of some bleak, more adult-oriented novels such as Aldous Huxley's vision of a genetically engineered and chemically pacified society, *Brave New World*, and George Orwell's *1984*, which has at its centre a forbidden love affair in a desolate future where everyone is tightly controlled by an omnipresent dictatorship. Roth explained to *USA Today* that people close to her were not expecting the more sinister elements of these influences to surface in her work: 'I think some people were surprised about the dark themes because I'm not a violent or a dark person.' She finished with a laugh, 'They know I'm not the book or vice versa. They got over it pretty quickly.'

When asked where the idea for *Divergent* came from, she explains it was a jumble of seemingly unrelated thoughts, images and theories that somehow merged together to form a complete whole. She was driving cross-state from her first school, Carleton College in Minnesota, to Northwestern University in Illinois and she found herself mesmerized by the tall buildings and cityscapes she saw on the way. She was haunted by the vision of someone jumping from the heights of a building, not by being forced or as an act of self-destruction, but as an exploit of courage or defiance. Roth was similarly intrigued by the idea of high-speed trains serving dual purposes as a necessary life-blood within a city, while also existing as an ever-present, menacing force. The author told the *Here & Now* radio show, 'They're almost like a creature. They move constantly, and it's not entirely clear who is driving them.'

Roth had grown up in Barrington, in the suburbs surrounding Chicago and had been a frequent visitor to the city. She realized the train images captured in her mind were a shadow of the long fascination she has with the public train system in Chicago (known locally as the 'El' due to the majority of the tracks being 'elevated' above street level). It was only after she had written most of the book that she understood the city she was creating as the representation of her dystopian world could easily be a reimagined, future version of the real Chicago. 'I have lived next to Chicago since I was five years old, so it is both familiar to me and unfamiliar, because I've never actually lived there,' she said to the Confessions of a Bookaholic blog. 'It is beautiful, clean, and orderly, which makes imagining it crumbling and falling apart at the seams all the more interesting.'

With the physical world of *Divergent* beginning to take shape, Roth started to incorporate some of the ideas she was studying in her psychology lectures (such as therapies intended to control and alter the thought processes that lead to anxiety and negative feeling) as well as some of her own religious convictions and ideas about basic human nature and moral values. Although Roth is a practising Christian and has spoken freely about faith and her own religious beliefs, her opinions on that subject have rarely infiltrated the pages of her books. She told Goodreads she was concerned about appearing too 'heavy-handed or preachy'.

When it came to the message and themes of the book, she said, 'The books I write are just explorations of things I'm thinking about, and my hope is that they make people think about them too.' She was more interested in the notion that some basic human character traits may not mean the same thing in every culture and why different societies hold certain characteristics in higher regard than others. She explained to the website, 'What I was exploring in *Divergent* is human nature and the ways in which it warps our best intentions and, on the flip side, how people sometimes rise to do good acts in the midst of chaos.'

She developed the idea of the separate factions that exist in the *Divergent* world as extensions of her own beliefs about human nature and our own society's pointless obsession with achieving perfection for perfection's sake. She told Amazon.com, 'I did spend a large portion of my adolescence trying to be as good as possible, so that I could prove my worth to the people around me, to myself, to God, to everyone.' She explained this further in an interview with MTV.com, saying, 'I would try to keep myself from doing anything wrong. I was trying to be the perfect child. That just created a lot of stress . . . Virtue and goodness, as an end unto themselves, when you're not using them out of love . . . can really become corrupted and evil.' She argued that being easily identifiable as a certain faction by your clothes, the style of your hair or even by your posture and body language were all intriguing concepts. 'I think we all secretly love and hate categories – love to get a firm hold on our identities, but hate to be confined. And I never loved and hated them more than when I was a teenager . . . we hear a lot about high school cliques, [but] I believe that adults categorize each other just as often, just in subtler ways.'

At first, Roth believed she was imagining a utopia – a society that appeared to be creating a better way of life – until it hit her that she was, in fact, creating a dystopia – a bleaker more oppressive universe, she revealed to Goodreads. '[The world I created] forced people to become narrower, twisted versions of themselves, and they ripped each other apart.' She joked, 'It was a really strange experience to realize that I would be a terrible God.' It was this potentially sinister aspect of forcing young people to choose a path in life based on fairly abstract aptitudes that would become the foundation of Roth's vision of the future. Although the society existing at the heart of the *Divergent* universe is seemingly more evolved than the one we would recognize today – there is no mention of prejudices based on race, religious beliefs, sexual orientation or political viewpoint – Roth was keen to admit, in some ways, her 'brave new world' was just as imperfect as the one we live in. 'A world in which you look different from the majority and no one minds? That sounds good to me,' she declared, before continuing, 'But when I think about it more, I realize that they're doing the exact same thing we do, but with different criteria by which to distinguish ourselves from others . . . Instead of skin colour, it's the colour of your shirt that people assess, or the results of your aptitude test. Same problem, different system.'

Roth admits, although she never had a completely mapped-out structure for the entire saga, she did have the definitive ending in mind from the very beginning, just in case she got the chance to write more than one book. A map might have been useful in those early days as Roth revealed her original draft of the story was told from the viewpoint of Four, the main male character. After writing a thirty-page outline, she hit a creative wall and abandoned the project. The incomplete manuscript was locked away, forgotten for nearly four years. While on her winter break, in the midst of completing her final year at university, Roth rediscovered the draft and realized she had the germ of an interesting story. Once she had made the simple switch to narrating from a female perspective, everything started to fall into place and Tris, Four and *Divergent* were born. She wrote the majority of the book in tandem with finishing her university course, working through the night and often penning sections of the book when she was supposed to be studying for tests or completing assignments. As a result, the book was written and virtually ready for publication before she graduated. Her main problem was that she hadn't been able to get any real interest for the manuscript from anyone inside the publishing industry. Instead, with no real job prospects, she was contemplating applying for another writing course to continue her studies.

Roth had also become disheartened and unsure about her choice to concentrate on writing within the young adult genre. She felt she should consider writing for the more lucrative – and straightforward – adult market, she told the American Library Association's Teens' Top Ten website. 'So many people had asked me if I was ever going to write for adults, which was sometimes a perfectly normal question and sometimes a condescending one, and I was starting to wonder if I should ignore my natural inclinations and try it.' Thankfully, she didn't, and the break she needed was just around the corner.

She had met an agent at a conference and asked her to take a look at what she'd written and offer advice. On the strength of what she read, the agent signed Roth as a client and sent the manuscript to several publishers. In less than a week, there was an offer on the table and Roth had signed a deal with HarperCollins to publish the book, with an option to create a whole series based around the characters and the world of *Divergent*. Her life had been turned upside down in the blink of an eye, she revealed to the Teens' Top Ten site. 'You could say the book changed everything . . . it began my career in writing, it gave me a new and different sense of purpose . . . my life is different now than it was before. I now have the distinct sense that I am standing in exactly the spot I should be standing in.'

The most important voice in the book is that of Beatrice 'Tris' Prior. She is not only the main character and narrator of the book, but she is the catalyst for virtually everything that happens in the story. It is her actions that shape the destiny of most of the other characters. Roth saw she was going to have to draw on something other than her own experiences to flesh out a realistic action heroine who was strong, independent and decisive enough to survive in some fairly extreme situations. She continued to the same website, 'Tris would say you have to learn how to run, fire a gun and jump on a train, but she lives in a different world.' She finished with a smile, 'The way I survive is by memorizing the order of the red line [train] stops, always put my keys in the same spot in my bag and wearing lots of layers so I don't freeze to death during the Chicago winters.'

Creating Tris would be Roth's biggest challenge and one she relished the most. She told the *Los Angeles Times* she wanted to create a powerful female character who, through the choices she makes for herself as the story unfolds, transforms from one thing to another. 'It's important that she starts out not a particularly brave character, or at least her bravery is downplayed and dormant. She is physically weak and small and everybody underestimates her,' adding, 'I think a lot of readers, especially teens, feel like they're in that situation too.'

She informed the BrodartVibe blog, 'With Tris, I struck a good balance of understanding her – so that I could write from her perspective comfortably – and not understanding her – so that I was motivated to learn more about her.' She appreciated the book depended on the plausibility of Tris and her reactions, continuing, 'Sometimes I would try to write the story another way, but it was like she wouldn't let me. I always had to go back to what Tris would choose, for better or for worse.' And as Roth had previously stated, this also meant Tris's love life would be refreshingly uncomplicated. She stressed the point to *USA Today*, saying, 'It's not really in her nature to be indecisive . . . Tris is just not the kind of character who would be divided in that way. For me, it was always clear that there was not going to be a love triangle for her,' justifying her choice with, '[It's] a little more interesting and challenging as a writer.'

It was becoming apparent that in *Divergent*'s Tris Prior, we were looking at a different kind of young adult heroine. The obvious comparison is with *The Hunger Games* and its main protagonist, Katniss Everdeen. Although Roth is quick to admit she is flattered by the comparison, she states it was never her intention to deliberately copy that particular book, or even explore similar themes. Above all, she believes that although they share some characteristics, Tris is different in many ways to Katniss, and not just in terms of her love life. She insists that, while many young adult heroines express their strength in a physical way, Katniss and Tris share a more intellectual and instinctual approach. She explained to the *Los Angeles Times*, 'Tris is physically weak but she learns how to be skilled in a physical way. Katniss isn't super buff, but she knows how to defend herself . . . their worth and strength is not limited to their physical abilities,' stating in that respect at least, 'They're very much in control of their own destinies.' She concluded that what did separate them was the subtle differences in their respective situations: Katniss has no control over her 'reaping' into the annual Hunger Games, whereas Tris is constantly faced with making her own choices, shaping her own future. 'Everything that happens, good or bad, happens because of the choice of the main character.'

Any well-rounded character has traits that will infuriate and baffle the reader, and Tris was no exception. Roth told *USA Today*, 'I don't think that people always love her . . . she makes some decisions that make you just want to shake her . . . she's young and she's just figuring herself out.' When the Best I've Read blog asked Roth to describe Tris in three words, she chose brave, incisive and impulsive. When asked to do the same for her main male character, Four, she decided on, thoughtful, strong and frustrating.

It is this last word which holds the key to the character of Four, and especially to the foundation of his relationship with Tris. Roth clarified the point to the *Los Angeles Times*: 'They're not without their problems and they have a complicated relationship.' Her wish to establish Four as an authority figure in Tris's new world becomes the catalyst for much of the initial conflict and eventual attraction that brings them together. Four is Tris's Dauntless training instructor, but he also shares several other important traits with her – he is an Abnegation transfer and, most importantly, he was similarly discovered to be Divergent. His frustration arises from seeing something special in Tris and knowing she has the potential to become more than she already is. Roth continued, '[Four] wants Tris to be strong and is attracted to her because of her strength . . . He always believes that she's stronger than she believes she is.' The fundamental connection between them is sparked by Four trying to help Tris recognize and harness her untapped inner strength, but Roth illustrates Four's real attraction to her comes when, during the Dauntless initiation process, he sees her becoming more vulnerable. Four admits to himself that he wants to feel the same thing and he realizes Tris is capable of helping him achieve it.

In creating a character who believes in encouragement and pushing someone to reach their full potential, rather than standing in their way and forcing them to make choices based on their needs, Roth sets Four apart from the likes of Edward Cullen or Jacob Black – they spend most of their time in the *Twilight* series trying to deny Bella what she wants or attempting to change her to suit their own ideas of who she should be.

Tris and Four's romance reflects Roth's own views on the subject, ardent their relationship should be built on mutual respect rather than a 'thunder-bolt' attraction or so-called destiny. She told *USA Today*, 'I had to think a lot about my teenage experience of love and just how you focus so much on all the little details.' She was keen to show she understood exactly what her readers were going through and aimed to reflect it in the book. 'I just tried to remember how exciting everything was when I was just falling in love.' It was this joyfulness and carefree aspect of falling for someone that Roth appreciated would need to shine through if the reader was to believe such a spark could ignite between these seemingly very different characters during what was undoubtedly a very turbulent and confusing period in their lives. Roth wanted her readers to see Tris and Four grow as separate individuals, but continue to choose each other amidst a series of challenging situations – without the interference of a love rival. The central romance had to be an anchor for the narrative, but Roth couldn't allow it to slow the momentum of the wider story she was telling. 'I think that romance is friendship and attraction sort of meeting together . . . It's important to show the characters having actual conversations about things other than their feelings for each other – and to develop their friendship on the page.' She concluded, 'All those things that I believe about relationships and what makes a healthy relationship really made it into the book.'

Since Roth had created quite an extensive history for Four in her abandoned first draft, she already had a fairly complete understanding of his personality before attempting to re-insert him back into the story. Although Roth admits to some similarities between herself and her main female protagonist, recognizing Tris as her entry point and guiding voice within the revised *Divergent* world, she would come to realize it was Four who had been instilled with more of her own basic characteristics. She states that although he likes to keep aspects of himself private, his openness and honesty is something she could relate to; it is this quality that gives him the air of confidence and the ability to speak his mind. 'He's pretty sure of himself in different ways . . . I think he's always certain of how he feels about Tris and he just doesn't think it's a big deal to tell her exactly what the experience he's having is.' It is this fearlessness to express his feelings and the certainty with which he approaches life that makes Four an ideal member of the Dauntless faction.

Four also enthusiastically embraces another important Dauntless characteristic, one which is integral to complete acceptance – he shares the faction's belief in tattoos and understands their significance within their view of society. Although Roth doesn't have any herself, she considers that in real life, as they are in the book, tattoos play an important part in defining individuality and celebrating life events and allegiances. She told the YA Highway website, 'I think a tattoo has to be meaningful, visually interesting, and something that will never change no matter what happens.' For Tris, getting her first tattoo became a symbol of her commitment to her future with Dauntless, as well as a tribute to her family and a reminder of her Abnegation past. Four has tattoos of all five factions, and this makes a much bolder statement. It proclaims his view that the faction system is deeply flawed and that people should be able to display the basic qualities of all the factions, rather than have to live under the limitations of just one. Tris and Four's tattoos would feature pointedly in some of the first poster art released to promote *Divergent*, acting as a powerful and intriguing first look at the real-life interpretations of the characters.

Roth had never really considered Hollywood would come knocking at her door or that turning her novel into a film would almost be an automatic process. She describes herself as more of a book person, telling NextMovie.com, 'I really just love books and I never really watch movies . . . I'm more into the slow, sort of meditative process and movies are like, "Bam-bam-bam!"' While she thinks the whole idea of someone wanting to adapt her book is flattering, she has strong views about book-to-movie adaptations, and was suitably apprehensive about this happening to *Divergent*. She told journalist Ben Falk in an interview for his website, 'I try to think of movies that are based on books as supplements to those books, not replacements . . . We get into trouble when we expect something in one format to match the other format perfectly – it's a new work, and it's allowed to be different.' She concluded, 'Some things that work on the page just don't work on screen, and for that reason I try to be forgiving when moviemakers alter things for the sake of the new medium.' When Falk asked if she had thought about the possibility of a film while she was writing the book, she replied, 'I barely had a book in mind when I was writing it!'

Roth believes there is a danger in writing books solely with the idea of turning it into a movie. 'Writing a book is such an involved process that it's hard to get through one if you love it for what it is, let alone if you're just writing one so it can be something else.' She illustrated her point by saying, 'This would be like becoming a supermodel just so that you can become a fashion designer,' explaining, 'becoming one is hard enough, let alone both, and they require a completely different set of skills.'

She discussed her own thought process further, admitting she did write with a certain cinematic eye. 'I do sort of think in "movie" . . . I let the scene play out in visual form in my head before I write it . . . but I never thought that my mental-movie-translated-to-words might be again translated into [an actual] movie.'

But that is exactly what happened, and it happened fast. Several months before the book had even hit the shelves, the film rights were snapped up by Summit Entertainment. Their involvement in adapting Stephenie Meyer's *Twilight* saga into one of the biggest movie series of all time turned them into one of the most important film studios in Hollywood. Eager to ride the wave of interest in young adult and supernatural fiction the *Twilight* films had left in their wake, the major film studios were falling over themselves to sign up the next big thing – thus reports started to flood in that movie adaptations of *The Hunger Games*, *The Mortal Instruments*, the Percy Jackson series and countless others were all in the pipeline. After the success of the *Twilight* movies, Summit were bought by Lionsgate, turning them into one of the most powerful studios in America, positioning them perfectly to take on the next big franchise.

Once the film rights had been acquired, Summit's first task was to find someone who would deliver a screenplay capturing the book's emotional centre and mirror the story's fast pace and breathtaking action sequences. When Roth was asked if she had considered writing the adaptation herself, she told the *Wall Street Journal*, 'I'm a book girl. I think it's interesting and certainly exciting [to write a screenplay], but it's not really what I want to be doing.' Apart from anything else, at the time Roth had her hands full writing the third instalment of the series, *Allegiant*. Although she stated she didn't want to get too involved, she said letting go completely was a scary thought and it was impossible not to worry about what direction a third party might take the story or her beloved characters. In the end, despite her other commitments, she made herself available for advice and guidance throughout the whole book-to-film process. She told NovelNovice.com, 'Part of it is shrinking something that is book size – and it's not a short book – and not cutting all the meat out of it. The challenge will be balancing the visual elements and the more meaningful things like fear and friendship and camaraderie.' She joked, 'I'm glad I'm not doing it.'

That honour would instead go to Evan Daugherty, a relative newcomer who had just scored a notable success as the writer of *Snow White and the Huntsman*, the re-imagining of the classic fairy tale starring Kristen Stewart and Chris Hemsworth. Daugherty spoke to Hypable.com, telling them what attracted him to the story: '[Tris] starts off in that incredibly sheltered, selfless, peaceful world and then basically she decides to join the equivalent of the Navy SEALs . . . that's a big character arc.'

The similarities of *Divergent* to his previous work are obvious: a strong female protagonist, a love story that blossoms between an unlikely couple (the Huntsman was, after all, supposed to hand an imprisoned Snow White over to the Evil Queen) and multiple story threads involving honour, complicated family relationships, finding inner courage and personal sacrifice. Roth remained respectfully removed from the process of writing the first draft, but the pair had met and maintained contact via e-mail. Roth told the Hollywood Crush blog at the time, 'I think he has a pretty good image of some of the places and characters, but some of them are a little iffy for him, so he's going to be asking me questions.' Eventually, Daugherty would share writing duties with Vanessa Taylor, a much more experienced television writer brought in at the second draft stage. Taylor's credentials include *Alias*, *Everwood* and more recently several episodes of the hugely popular HBO series, *Game of Thrones*. It was obvious she would help with the pacing of the script, as well as injecting a more authentic human edge into the more science fiction-based elements of the story.

When Roth finally got a chance to see a version of the screenplay, she told Hypable.com she was suitably blown away with the work of the two writers. 'I've never read a script before. I was really impressed by how closely it stuck to the general plot line of the book.' As the script looked like it was nearing completion, Roth was relieved everything was coming together relatively painlessly and she remained excited to see the universe she had created materialize in front of her. She said, 'Everyone seems really positive and pumped up and excited to figure out the details of this crazy world.'

One of the most important elements in that 'crazy world' would be the actors who had been hired to play Tris and Four. Roth had been quick to counter any negative sentiment that had arisen after the casting of Shailene and Theo. She wasn't going to listen to any nonsense about someone being too old, the age difference or the fact that someone just might be too good looking. After the first screen test showed the true star qualities of the two leads, Roth told *USA Today*, 'It was pretty nuts seeing Theo and Shailene acting together for the first time . . . they were in a blank room, sitting in chairs, obviously not in costume, not with sets around them. I still felt they were exactly right.' She concluded, 'They were Tris and Four instead of Shailene and Theo and that's pretty incredible because I wasn't sure at that point if we would be able to find anyone who could capture those characters just right . . . but it was amazing, and they had great chemistry.'

Veronica Roth's version of the *Divergent* world was undoubtedly vivid, but to make it truly come alive and become a reality on the big screen, she would inevitably have to hand the reins over to someone else. The search was on to find a director who not only understood her vision, but also had their own thoughts on the story. Roth would end up entrusting her creation to filmmaker Neil Burger.

Burger's journey to the world of *Divergent* was a relatively straightforward one. He had graduated with a fine arts degree from Yale University and, after a brief period making experimental films in the 1980s, went on to create music videos for alternative rock bands. This, in turn, led to him working on a series of short films for MTV promoting reading in young adults. From there, he entered the world of directing commercials, which he did for several years with the acclaimed Ridley Scott Associates. This experience had given him many transferable skills, he told *Variety*: 'Commercials were a wonderful training ground because you were able to work in every situation – with kids, special effects, blue-screens, dogs, helicopters.' His first film, released in 2002, was a mock documentary, *Interview with the Assassin*, which won the Best Feature award at the Woodstock Film Festival and was nominated for several Independent Spirit Awards. This was followed by *The Illusionist* in 2006, a high-profile project with a much larger budget of $17 million, starring Edward Norton, Jessica Biel and Paul Giamatti. The film explores the thin line that exists between truth and illusion, blurring the boundaries between reality and the supernatural. It was released in the same year as Christopher Nolan's *The Prestige*, which dealt with similar subject matter, and it is generally thought that both films suffered at the box office as a result of this scheduling clash. Burger's next film was *The Lucky Ones*, a road movie involving three soldiers on a drive from New York to Las Vegas after returning home from active duty. The film was considered a substantial flop, making only $300,000 from an estimated $14 million budget, and was removed from cinemas after just one week of release. It would be three years before Burger would direct another major film. 2011's *Limitless* starred a fast-rising Bradley Cooper, still hot from the success of *The Hangover*, and industry veteran Robert De Niro. Cooper plays a writer who, while suffering an extended period of writer's block, uses an experimental drug with mind-enhancing properties, which helps him unlock his brain's full potential. He not only finishes his book, he makes a fortune on the stock market in the process. The film was a surprise box-office hit, taking in more than $160 million in the US from a reported $27 million budget. It delivered Cooper his first big hit as a lead actor and paved the way for his Oscar-nominated role in *Silver Linings Playbook* in 2012.

If *Limitless* had proven Burger could deliver a sophisticated-looking movie from a relatively small budget, then *The Illusionist* had shown he knew how to handle a film based on a recognizable reality interwoven with many fantastic elements. Both these abilities would be instrumental in his landing the role as director of *Divergent.*

With the first draft script in hand, Burger was keen to flesh out his new world, and he was eager to get as much detail as possible 'straight from the horse's mouth'. Roth remembers the countless discussions about many of the finer points of the fractured society she had created. She recalled, in an interview with Hypable.com, 'Everything down to the little details that I saw have been well thought out, [even] the philosophy of the world. [Burger] and I talked for hours – he asked me so many questions, things I never thought of. Like, "How does commerce work in this particular faction?" I was like, "I don't know! Where were you when I was writing this?"' She finished, 'Those conversations were really reassuring because he's been so interested in every little thing.'

With the book in reassuringly safe hands and all the key ingredients falling into place, it was time for the cast and crew to start the daunting process of actually building the *Divergent* world. It was a real leap into the unknown and it was going to be challenging. It was time for everyone, including Shailene and Theo, to unleash their inner Dauntless and enter their own fear landscape at last.

Chapter Eleven

SHAILENE AND THEO: DIVERGENT TOGETHER

FINDING THE RIGHT PEOPLE TO PLAY all the key roles in *Divergent*
was a full-time job, but, ever so slowly, an impressive array of
acting talent was assembled as the cast was finalized. Over the
next few weeks, it seemed no internet entertainment news feed
was complete without a daily announcement involving someone
landing a crucial part in the *Divergent* universe. First, Kate Winslet
was confirmed to play Erudite leader Jeanine Matthews, then in
quick succession came stories that Maggie Q would play tattoo
artist Tori, Zoë Kravitz would take on the role of Tris's initiate
friend, Christina, Ansel Elgort would be Tris's brother Caleb and
Jai Courtney was on board as Dauntless leader Eric. Eventually, the
cast was complete and the entire crew headed to Chicago to start
filming in early March 2013. The shoot was reported to last sixty
days and the movie had what was deemed a fairly tight budget of
$40 million.

Prior to the location shoot, many of the principal cast

members, including all the Dauntless initiates, were subjected to a fairly rigorous and extensive physical training programme. This would involve stamina and fitness exercises, fight training (featuring an intensive martial arts programme), working with weapons including knives and guns, and even taking part in a survival course that equipped them with the basic knowledge for eventualities such as making fires, building shelters and finding drinking water. It may sound like they were preparing them for a real life Hunger Games, but this comprehensive preparation would prove to be invaluable. Not only did it ready them physically and mentally for the upcoming months of filming, it meant that all the actors had started to forge the bonds that would help them convincingly portray the relationships that existed between the various characters. *Divergent* author Veronica Roth couldn't help notice this bond during her first of many set visits, telling the Hypable website, 'It's really interesting to see how the actual actor relationships reflect the character relationships. All the young initiates have a great camaraderie with each other.'

Director Neil Burger had said in order to ground the movie in reality and give it the edgier look he required, he would be filming in as many real locations as possible. Inspired by Christopher Nolan's use of the city as a stand-in for Gotham City in his acclaimed *Dark Knight* trilogy, Burger was convinced the real Chicago would perfectly fit Roth's vision. Roth had expressed her initial concerns, and ultimate relief, to Hypable.com, stating, 'I was worried that the overall sense of the movie would be a little too futuristic [and] sexy . . . sleek and shiny. That's not the world of *Divergent*.' She quickly praised the director's choices, saying, 'Everything's falling apart [in the book], and I think [Neil Burger] definitely [captured] that. The visuals I've seen have been in that vein.' Burger told EW.com, 'Every movie these days they're like, "Let's shoot this in Canada or Louisiana or Romania because it's cheaper." I didn't want digital landscapes or CGI skylines. This is great for the story and it's great for Chicago and it's great for the movie.' His goal was to achieve something that would set it apart from the digitally created Panem in *The Hunger Games* or the heavily CGI-based design of much of *Beautiful Creatures*. Only by successfully achieving this would the film's visual style attain Burger's vision and match what he described as 'the energy and the rawness of the way we're telling the story'.

Some sets were built within the Chicago city limits, allowing them to maintain the required real-world Chicago skylines. Roth, a frequent visitor to these newly constructed locations, was suitably impressed with what she saw, she told EW.com. 'That first day I think I just stared at everything for five hours and couldn't even form a sentence.' Roth would later tell the 2013 Comic-Con audience, 'When I write, I don't have the most detailed mind . . . seeing [the scenes] realized in an incredibly detailed way is really wonderful . . . all the set pieces are just so wonderfully crafted.' She concluded, 'to me it's really true to the book and it's also a surprise, which is a wonderful combination.'

The complicated shooting schedule wasn't going to ease anyone in gently. Some of the first scenes to be filmed were action-packed moments from Tris's early initiation tasks, taking place shortly after she arrives at the Dauntless training compound. First up was capturing the moment when Tris and her fellow initiates must take a terrifying leap-of-faith from the ledge of a tall building into a deep, pitch-black chasm, which serves as the entrance to the Dauntless encampment – they must show their allegiance to their new faction with a literal step into the unknown. The scene was filmed on the roof of a converted retail warehouse, the Spiegel building, a landmark building in the South Side of the city. Although the reality of the situation was a lot safer than the incident portrayed in the book, there were still precautions to be taken. Burger told *Entertainment Weekly*, 'We've been nervously planning it because it is dangerous and there's a lot of people on the roof . . . We had to pull it off safely and also pull it off cinematically, so you have this knot in your stomach as you watch this young woman decide to do this crazy thing.'

It became clear very early on that all of the cast were going to be put through their paces, but none more so than Shailene and Theo. Burger had nothing but praise for his actors, stating that even in these introductory scenes he had come to realize his assembled group of young stars were ready to rise to any challenge, and was impressed with how committed they were to the hard work that was undoubtedly ahead. He singled out Shailene as the perfect example of the can-do spirit spreading through the entire production. 'Shailene says she's not afraid of heights but that she's afraid of falling . . . but she really did stand on that ledge.' He finished, 'She's incredibly game and so adventurous. In a way, she's very Dauntless.'

The first scene in the book that really shows a development in Tris and Four's relationship takes place during a night-time 'capture the flag' group exercise. It is one of the most important scenes in the book – and potentially the most visually arresting in the film – and unfolds on a giant ferris wheel in an abandoned fairground. A key action set piece, it also signals the first time Tris truly feels she has been accepted by the other initiates, as well as being a pivotal moment in the evolution of her bond with Four. During their time alone together as they climb the wheel,

Four admits he has a fear of heights and begins to open up to Tris, revealing a hidden, more vulnerable side. This was the scene that had initially attracted Theo to the role of Four, and he revealed to the San Diego Comic-Con crowd it was one of the things he liked most about the book. 'When they're on the ferris wheel and he's afraid of heights and Tris says, "What, are you scared of heights?" and he doesn't shy away from it, he says, "Yeah, of course I am. You can't be afraid of nothing; everyone's afraid of something."' He explained it was this openness he connected with, 'And that's the concept that I loved: bravery is not about being fearless, it's about how you deal with the things that are scary and fear in itself, how you [deal] with things in the face of fear.'

The first image released to the press from the production was a still from the knife-throwing scene that takes place during the initiates' Dauntless weapons training sessions. It is another key moment in the growing relationship between Tris and Four, and in the film it would also be one of the first instances to demonstrate the amazing on-screen understanding between Shailene and Theo, only hinted at in early photo shoots and interviews. In the book, during the initiates' second weapons training session, Al, one of the other transfers, has trouble hitting the target with his knife. As a punishment, he is forced to stand in front of a target while Four throws knives at him. Tris volunteers to take Al's place, an act that is seen as kind, selfless and brave as she is now confronted with her own fear as she faces Four's knives herself. She succeeds in doing so, but is left shocked and deeply shaken when Four, after goading her to give up, throws the last knife at the target, slightly cutting her ear and drawing blood. Tris realizes he wounded her on purpose and stays behind after training to confront him. This is the first scene in which Four tries to let Tris know he is aware of her potential to succeed and that he, too, is Divergent.

Veronica Roth admitted to the Comic-Con audience that she didn't want to watch the filming of any 'smoochy' scenes between Shailene and Theo, because 'that's just awkward . . . voyeuristic somehow'. However, over time, she did catch moments of their performances as she visited the set, saying, 'I kept seeing slow development', and, she revealed in an interview with the Hollywood Crush blog, 'It was amazing. The chemistry was incredible, and he did a great job with the kind of sensitive, strong Four . . . it's just going to be awesome.'

Several of the most memorable action sequences in the first book involve the virtual reality simulations initiates must enter in order to face – and defeat – their most deep-seated nightmares. Only by conquering them can they prove they are truly fit for Dauntless and ready to join the faction. As they get to know one another better and Four opens up to Tris, he takes her through his own 'fear landscape' and in the process reveals his name stems from the fact he only had to face, and conquer, four challenges – a fear of heights, claustrophobia, an aversion to taking anyone's life and the trauma caused by the memory of his father beating him as a child. Tris is revealed to have seven fears, including being trapped in an enclosed space and drowning. She must face this latter fear in reality in the final stages of the book, but during her simulation, overcoming her fear and accepting that it is only an artificial representation would be an important moment in Tris's final transformation and empowerment – allowing her to fully embrace her Divergent nature and understand the power it gave her to challenge everything she had been forced to believe about the divided society she had grown up in.

Screenwriter Evan Daugherty commented to Bookish.com,

'The simulations provide some of the bigger challenges. For cinematic references, Christopher Nolan did such a cool job in *Inception* with the rich world of dreams that looked real but weren't quite real . . . you want them to be scary and you want them to feel real.' On watching the filming of these scenes, Veronica Roth exclaimed, 'I remember being really surprised by the water tank . . . I kind of forgot about it and then I saw the tank being filled with actual water and Shailene swimming in it and I was like, "Oh, my god."' Shailene was at home in the water and had shown as much in *The Descendants*, but being trapped in a glass box was a completely different matter. In the end, filming the scene went smoothly and Shailene's performance captured her obvious initial terror before she succumbs to an almost meditative state, unleashing her Divergent nature, which had been becoming increasingly prevalent as the story progressed. Tris realizes only she has the power to defeat her own weaknesses and with the help of her Dauntless training, she resourcefully makes her escape.

By mid-July 2013, with the majority of principle photography complete, Burger retreated to his editing suite and started to cut together some of the raw footage he had shot in Chicago. It was basic stuff, but because the film was not relying on computer-generated locations and backgrounds it meant he had more finished shots than most big action movies would have at that stage. There was an air of self-enforced urgency because the studio had announced that a large *Divergent* contingency would be attending Comic-Con International in San Diego to unveil the first completed footage to a rabid fan-packed audience in just a matter of days.

Comic-Con had started life as a small gathering of like-minded comic, movie and science fiction fans who wanted to create southern California's first comic book convention. Over the last forty years it has grown to become one of the biggest and most important launch pads for all kinds of projects, no longer restricted to solely science fiction and fantasy – from comic books and games to cult television shows and multi-million-dollar movies – the annual weekend conference now boasts attendances of over 130,000 visitors. Thanks to webcasts and live blogging, the event is a truly worldwide phenomenon and everybody working in film and television now knows Comic-Con can greatly influence the success or failure of any endeavour. Ongoing series have used the Comic-Con buzz to build their audience from cult to genuine ratings hits and falling viewing figures can be boosted between seasons by using the event to introduce new stars and writers, or by hinting at plot twists that might bring deserting fans back on board. A 'first look' trailer launch or a panel question and answer session at Comic-Con is now viewed as the most valuable (and cost effective) method to ignite the initial spark of interest in new projects among the all-important core fan base. In the last few years, major movie studios such as Marvel have seen Comic-Con as phase one of the marketing campaigns for all of their major releases and the event has managed to attract some of the biggest stars in the business, including Robert Downey Jr. and the entire *Avengers* cast in 2010. Initial buzz at Comic-Con has helped brand new series such as *Marvel's Agents of S.H.I.E.L.D.* and *Sleepy Hollow*, as well as returning shows like *The Walking Dead* deliver record-breaking television viewing ratings in the US in 2013.

Veronica Roth had been to Comic-Con as part of a Summit panel a couple of years earlier to promote *Divergent* and announce the movie adaptation. She told the Novel Novice website how she had been sandwiched between two *Twilight* panel sessions, thinking, 'I don't know how I'm gonna follow this act', but that the crowd had greeted her warmly on that occasion and she was in no doubt the reception this time would be similarly enthusiastic. Theo had also already attended Comic-Con as part of panels for *Underworld: Awakening* and the US launch of *Bedlam*, but this was Shailene's first trip – it's unlikely that many of the Comic-Con hardcore followed *The Secret Life of the American Teenager* or even were much interested in *The Descendants* when *Mission: Impossible – Ghost Protocol* and *Sherlock Holmes: A Game of Shadows* were playing in the screens next door. She was excited to get her first real feedback from the fans, and find out once and for all if they would accept her as their beloved Tris.

The *Divergent* session took place in the famous 6,500 capacity conference room known as Hall H. Joining Shailene and Theo on the panel were Roth and Burger, as well as many of the actors playing the key supporting characters – Mekhi Phifer as Max, Maggie Q, Miles Teller, Ansel Elgort, Zoë Kravitz, Ben Lloyd-Hughes (Will), Christian Madsen, Amy Newbold (Molly) and Ben Lamb (Edward). If the crowd weren't to be impressed by the fame of the actors, they were certainly going to be wowed by the quantity!

Roth opened the panel by outlining to the crowd the basic premise of her book, joking, when asked to explain the factions, 'It would be really bad if I couldn't remember them all right now!' In the end, there was no doubt the packed room were impressed with what they saw and they greeted the first-look footage with obvious excitement. Underlining the possible benefits a Comic-Con appearance can afford, and the consequent necessity of making sure a production has material to entice the fans, Burger was quick to stress the crew had only finished shooting the film two days earlier, saying, 'It's all very, very fresh for us right now . . . while we were shooting, we knew we were coming here and we wanted to come and show you guys something.' The reel Burger had put together received rapturous applause and Roth used this wave of positivity to give the book fans in the crowd (and watching all over the world) the first titbit of information about the soon to be published third book, *Allegiant*, telling the crowd the story would be told, in alternate chapters, from both Tris and Four's points of view.

It was then the two main stars' turn, and Shailene and Theo started off by speaking about their characters and the general look and feel of the film. After Theo had told the crowd, 'we really worked our asses off to make something that I think you'll all really be proud of . . . It's a really special movie and it has a really iconic look to it', panel host, US comedian Chris Hardwick, teased that listening to his English accent had just got 'half the room pregnant'. The general atmosphere could best be described as informal, upbeat and positive, which certainly boded well for the film.

When the audience question and answer session began it was obvious the crowd had been won over by what they'd seen and the questions came thick and fast, inevitably ending up focusing on the relationship between Shailene and Theo. Theo joked elements of his on-screen relationship with Shailene were all too real: 'I'm extremely protective of Shai by nature', he said, before adding, more straight-faced, 'I won't even let her go to the bathroom without me . . . it can be problematic, but I think I should be there if she needs protecting.'

This was also Roth's first chance to view finished footage cut together on a big screen, and when asked what it was like seeing it all come to life in front of her, she said, 'The experience is wonderful. When I write I don't have the most detailed mind . . . so I'm kind of squinting and looking at things that are blurry and far away, and seeing them actually realized in an incredibly detailed way was really wonderful.' She was especially relieved that although she recognized the world she had created, the film had its own very distinctive look. 'All the set pieces were so lovingly crafted by our wonderful crew . . . it's very true to the book, and also a surprise, so kind of a rare combination.'

The event was seen as a massive success and served as the perfect first step in the long and complicated journey that lay ahead before the film's eventual release. Unlike many big blockbuster movies that have taken to the Comic-Con stage over two or three consecutive years, from initial announcement and conception through to the final release, the *Divergent* crew wouldn't get another bite at the cherry: the film would be released long before the next Comic-Con in July 2014.

The next chapter in the gradual unveiling of the *Divergent* world was going to be at the annual Video Music Awards in LA on 25 August 2013.

A sneak peek at Comic-Con might be considered 'preaching to the converted', while the showing of the teaser trailer during the VMAs pre-show would be the first chance for a potential wider audience to get a glimpse of Shailene and Theo in action. If the movie was to become a success on the scale of *Twilight* or *The Hunger Games*, it would need to capture the general public's imagination as well as that of the science fiction and fantasy fans or the curious devotees of the original books.

Shailene and Theo walked the red carpet together. Theo wore a fairly casual John Varvatos suit and black shirt, while Shailene was wearing a beautiful blue and gold-fringed Emilio Pucci Resort mini skirt and a simple black crop top that exposed her impressive post-*Divergent* training abs. As well as showing off her newly toned stomach, this would be her first public appearance sporting her newly cropped hair. Unlike Anne Hathaway or Charlize Theron, it was less of a fashion statement for Shailene. She was only one week away from starting filming *The Fault In Our Stars*, in which she would play Hazel Lancaster, a seventeen-year-old girl who is fighting stage four cancer. She had decided she didn't want to wear wigs for the role and insisted the best way to convincingly portray the effects of the illness, and its treatment, was to cut off her long hair. She had posted photos of the real hair cutting session on Instagram and Twitter earlier that week with the title 'work in progress' and the hashtag '#itgrowsback' and, as always, Shailene saw this as a great opportunity to promote a worthwhile cause. She announced she would be donating her hair to a non-profit-making charity called Children With Hair Loss – the charity uses donated human hair to make wigs for people who need them. She told her Twitter followers, 'If you are in a position to cut off eight inches of your hair, then I strongly urge you to do it.' She continued, 'There are so many human beings out there who would LOVE the opportunity to possess long hair, but simply cannot because of their current situation. Let's share!'

When asked about her new haircut on the red carpet she said, 'I feel lighter. I also feel strong, especially when I'm able to cut it the way I want to cut it. I'm not nervous at all. So excited. I love it.'

Their main red carpet duty was to present the teaser trailer for *Divergent*. Introducing the clip, Shailene insisted the film had something new to offer: 'I think people will be very enthused by how it looks visually – very different from a lot of other young adult films.'

Further down the carpet, Miles Teller – who plays Peter in

Divergent – was also spreading the word. 'I would say that if you read the book, which a lot of people have, that it's very true to the book, so you'll see a lot of stuff that you'll remember, a lot of action. It's a big movie.'

After they had introduced the trailer during the pre-show, Shailene and Theo took their seats. Shailene started a few tongues wagging by sitting beside her former *Spectacular Now* co-star Teller, rather than Theo, suggesting the pair had become close during filming. Perez Hilton commented in his report the next day, 'We watched as the two rising stars took turns wrapping their arms around each other's shoulders and cracking each other up. While all that might be nothing, it was definitely cute.'

While *The Hunger Games* had used the VMAs as their launch platform in 2012 to startling effect, kick-starting a promotional campaign that built the anticipation for the movie to fever pitch, no one could have predicted the only thing anyone would be talking about on the morning of 26 August 2013 was a former Disney Channel teen star, her protruding tongue and a giant foam hand.

As Miley Cyrus strutted her stuff on the VMA stage, her performance building to a crescendo, it was clear a popular culture phenomenon was taking place. Reactions to Cyrus's 'twerking' and controversial dance moves instantly lit up internet comment boards and it wasn't long before Facebook and Twitter went into meltdown over what users had witnessed. Her set became a worldwide pop culture event and the next day every news channel, news website and newspaper ran a story on the VMAs' most infamous moment to date. Unfortunately for the *Divergent* crew, they had been well and truly overshadowed.

Although the whole experience must have been a slight disappointment for the cast and crew present, the *Divergent* machine was now up and running, and Burger and his team slipped out of sight and got down to the mammoth task at hand – completing their blockbuster movie franchise. They spent the next few months putting the finishing touches to the film, with post-production continuing into early 2014.

The first official trailer, with finished effects shots, was released in mid-November and incited an overwhelming response from fans. By the end of the month, Hypable.com announced that Hans Zimmer was working with Dutch producer and remixer Junkie XL (whose real name is Tom Holkenborg, the man most famous for his number-one remix of Elvis Presley's 'A Little Less Conversation' in 2002) on a score for the film. Lionsgate president Erik Feig revealed to the website that Zimmer, 'wants to do a superhero theme for a woman', giving a strong indication as to the possible sound of the movie.

In the meantime, the world of *Divergent* was pushed front and centre by the release of the third and final instalment of the saga, *Allegiant*, on 22 October 2013. As Veronica Roth had already announced at Comic-Con in July, this book would differ from the previous instalments in that it would be told from both Tris and Four's points of view, in alternate chapters, and readers' eagerness to see how it would all end resulted in the book breaking sales records for its publisher HarperCollins. Selling nearly 500,000 copies on its first day, *Allegiant* topped multiple charts, while the two previous instalments also experienced a correlating sales spike. The critical response to the book was mixed, but it was the fans' feedback that mattered most to Roth. On the whole, they were more than satisfied with the concluding episode in their beloved saga, but a minority reacted angrily to the book's controversial ending.

Eager to make sure the fans understood her motives, Roth used her own blog to explain her choices. 'I've said before that this ending was a part of the plan, but one thing I want to make clear is that I didn't choose it to shock anyone, or to upset anyone.' She insisted the finale mirrored the overall theme that had initially surfaced in the first book, where 'a moment of triumph [is] followed by a moment of total devastation', which in turn had led Tris to fully understand what it meant to be Divergent – 'combining selflessness and bravery and love for her family and love for her faction all together'.

Roth's time in the literary world of *Divergent* was almost over. She planned to keep the momentum building to the film's release with the publication of four short stories told from Four's perspective, following the previously released e-book *Free Four* from April 2012. Thus, *The Transfer*, *The Initiate*, *The Son* and *The Traitor* would be released at regular intervals during late 2013 and early 2014 and would fill in backstory and explore previously unseen events from the *Divergent* books. The stories would be released separately as e-books and then published in a combined print format in February 2014. The baton would then be passed, and it would be the fast-approaching film adaptation that would be charged with keeping the *Divergent* legacy alive.

Chapter Twelve

SHAILENE AND THEO: A LEAP INTO THE UNKNOWN

WHEN ASKED BY THE WHATCHA READING NOW? website where she would like to go if she could transport herself back to any time or place in history, Veronica Roth protested, 'Do I have to go back? The future is uncertain and full of possibilities, so I'm more interested in seeing that.' Roth had finished the next two books in the series and, with the set of short stories centred round the character of Four acting as a final epilogue, contemplated a life outside the world of *Divergent*. It was a daunting prospect and Roth was quick to admit to *Here & Now* radio that 'It's very bittersweet . . . I'm happy to let go of these secrets and for everyone to know how this story ends, but the series has been special to me. It's changed my life. And I have a deep affection for these characters . . . I'm going to have to mope a little bit after this.' Like J K Rowling, Stephenie Meyer and Suzanne Collins before her, Roth was now in the unenviable position of trying to meet the ongoing expectations of her avid and loyal fan base. Asked by *USA*

Today, 'What's next?' she replied, 'I know I'll be writing for young adults for a long time. Mostly because I just love the readers and the teachers and the librarians that I interact with . . . I have a few ideas, but nothing really solid.' One thing is for sure: the spirit of the *Divergent* world Roth has created will live on in the hearts and minds of the millions of loyal readers, and in the movie adaptation that is sure to capture hordes of new fans.

As for Theo, his name was still on everyone's lips. In autumn 2013, the news that Charlie Hunnam had dropped out of the planned movie of *Fifty Shades of Grey*, citing worries about the film's proposed script and a fear of committing to a possible franchise, meant the search for someone to fill Christian Grey's shoes was back on. Theo had been mentioned during the initial round of casting rumours as part of a very long list of possibilities, before Hunnam was eventually confirmed in the role, yet here he was again in countless web articles and newspaper columns, now on a much shorter list alongside frontrunner Jamie Dornan. In the end it was Dornan who won the part, but it stands as a clear indication of just how far Theo's star had risen during the summer of 2013 that he was talked of for such a high profile character.

Instead of *Fifty Shades*, Theo's schedule was packed with smaller projects, the first of which was *London Fields*, a film adaptation of Martin Amis's 1989 novel. The movie stars Billy Bob Thornton as a terminally ill author who has suffered severe writer's block for the last twenty years. Theo would join a cast that included Amber Heard and Jim Sturgess as it began shooting in London in September 2013.

Within a matter of weeks Theo was also signed to star alongside Dakota Fanning and Richard Gere in the low budget indie drama, *Franny*, which was set to start shooting in Philadelphia in late

October 2013. The film, written and directed by newcomer Andrew Rcnzi, tells the story of an older man (Gere) who manages to entangle himself in the lives of a young couple (Theo and Fanning) in an attempt to relive his past.

Theo had one more project in the pipeline; a Christmas comedy called *The Most Wonderful Time* that would again see him work with big industry names. Alan Arkin, Diane Keaton, Annette Bening and Amanda Seyfried were all in talks, at the time of writing, to star in the film that would be directed by Jessie Nelson (*I Am Sam* and *Stepmom*), from a screenplay penned by Steven Rogers, famous as the go-to screenwriter of romantic comedies, including *Hope Floats* and *P.S. I Love You*.

It is clear Theo's career is going from strength to strength as he moves rapidly up through the Hollywood pecking order and, like Robert Pattinson before him, he has started reaping the many rewards that come with being attached to a potential blockbuster franchise. The perks arising from this heightened profile are obvious – working with inspiring directors and new writers, getting the chance to hold his own alongside respected actors such as Billy Bob Thornton, Richard Gere and Annette Bening, proving he deserves to be ranked equally with critically acclaimed, up-and-coming talents like Dakota Fanning and Jim Sturgess, as well as now being in the enviable position of being able to be more picky when it comes to projects he is offered. He may have taken his time making up his mind about fully committing to acting, but it is with true Dauntless determination that he stuck to the decision that has set him on a path that will allow him to achieve great things in the future.

As far back as February 2012, Shailene had made it clear that her post-*Secret Life* career was not going to follow the path typically taken by the average young TV starlet turning her attention to movies, telling Examiner.com, 'I would like to do something dark or small. I love independent films. I love emotional scenes. I love people who are struggling with something.' It's safe to say that she has been true to her word and, following the positive critical response towards her work in *The Descendants*, Shailene has shown a rare fearlessness in her choice of projects.

Her first job after the completion of *Divergent* wouldn't be any different. Before embarking upon her journey to take Tris Prior from page to screen, Shailene had become fascinated with the idea of portraying another strong literary role in the adaptation of John Green's best-selling novel, *The Fault In Our Stars*. While not as physically demanding as her time spent as Tris, it would take Shailene out of her comfort zone and provide the challenges she so craved, as she would be playing sixteen-year-old Hazel Grace Lancaster, a terminally ill sufferer of stage four cancer. Coincidentally, it was a book *Divergent* author Veronica Roth herself had read a good six months before Shailene had even been cast as Tris. In *USA Today* she described it as 'meaningful and powerful', and told Claire Zulkey in a radio interview on WBEZ 91.5, 'It struck a good balance between emotion and humour, and it made me very thoughtful for several days, which is a sign of a good book, for me.'

Having also read Scott Neustadter and Michael H. Weber's script, the writers she had worked with and loved on *The Spectacular Now*, Shailene revealed to the Hollywood Crush blog, 'I read the book and fought really, really hard for [the part of Hazel]'. She stressed how much it meant to her, saying, '[I] basically said no matter what I do, I will do anything to be in this movie, even if I audition for Hazel and they're like, "No, you're not her", I just really want to be an extra because I'm so passionate about it.' She eventually won the role in March 2013, explaining, 'Finally, when they cast the director, I auditioned for him, and I guess he liked what I did because I got it.'

Relative unknown Josh Boone was to be that director, and his reaction to casting Shailene was a little more enthusiastic than she implies. His search to fill the role of Hazel had been exhaustive. 'I saw some stunning auditions . . . over 250 girls read for the part, but it wasn't until Shailene stepped in front of the camera that I truly saw Hazel for the first time.' He continued, 'She just killed it. She did a phenomenal job. We were all crying.'

Boone's only previous feature film, 2012's family drama *Stuck in Love*, had been a modest critical success, but his realistic handling of the family's relationships and the film's balance of comedy, drama and romance, along with his personal connection to the subject matter, meant he was perfect to handle the more harrowing elements of *The Fault In Our Stars*. He revealed to EW.com, 'I had a close friend who died of stage four lung cancer . . . the book helped me through a rough patch. It does it with a smile and witty cynicism.'

The book's author, John Green, was similarly thrilled by Shailene, telling EW.com, 'It means a lot to me that she is a fan of the book, and I know from our conversations that she has a profound understanding of Hazel.' He then admitted, upon happening to see her first audition, 'I felt like Hazel Grace Lancaster was talking to me. It was eerie, and very exciting.'

Also joining the cast of *The Fault In Our Stars* was Ansel Elgort as Augustus Waters, the male lead who is facing an even tougher battle with cancer than Hazel. He had been Shailene's co-star in *Divergent*, playing Tris's brother, Caleb. After initial worries that the audience would find it difficult to accept him as Shailene's brother and then her boyfriend within a matter of months, the film's producer, Wyck Godfrey, said to EW.com, 'His performance completely annihilated our concerns . . . We were all swept away by the humour, charm and aching vulnerability Ansel brings to his portrayal.' He finished, 'we are confident that fans of *Fault* will fall in love with him the same way that Hazel does – slowly, and then all at once.'

Shailene was in no way worried about the situation, as she joked with Elgort on the set of *Divergent*, telling him, 'In a few months, buddy, you're going to be my lover.' In another interview, with Hypable.com, she was a little more serious about his qualities. 'He blew it out the water. He's a real sweetheart. I'm so excited to have him in my life.' Ansel was quick to state he felt both he and Shailene had the necessary skills to make the leap from depicting a sibling relationship to a romantic one successful: 'I think that's the magic of being an actor . . . you can do that and it's not weird.' He emphatically concluded, 'I feel like Shailene is the best actress I've ever met . . . and I feel like I'm a pretty good actor, too, so I think it's going to be no problem for us. It'll be great . . . acting is acting.'

Production took place in Pittsburgh, Pennsylvania during the late summer of 2013, with principle photography completed by mid-October. *The Fault In Our Stars* is due for release in the US on 6 June 2014, less than three months after *Divergent*'s debut. This pattern – blockbuster young adult adaptation followed by an illness-themed comedy/drama – mimics the double box office punch delivered by Jennifer Lawrence in 2012 with the back-to-back release of *The Hunger Games* and *Silver Linings Playbook*. Let's not forget Lawrence took home an Oscar for her role in the latter, and it must serve as a promising omen that Shailene will, at last, get the Oscar nomination she so richly deserves and surprisingly missed out on for *The Descendants*.

As 2013 came to a close, 20th Century Fox released the first poster for *The Fault In Our Stars*, featuring a simple image of Shailene and Ansel Elgort lying cheek-to-cheek on a background of lush grass. John Green spoke about the picture's depiction of Shailene wearing her character's oxygen tubes to EW.com: 'A major Hollywood studio released a movie poster in which the female romantic lead has visible evidence of her disability, which is damn near unprecedented, and I'm thrilled they put her face – and her [oxygen tubes] – on the poster.' It was the promotional piece's tagline – 'One Sick Love Story' – that was causing a little more controversy and debate. It may appear in slightly poor taste and out of step with the book's subject matter, and Green initially used his blog to say, 'I did not write the tag line. To the many of you who love it, I say, "I did not write the tag line." To the many of you who don't, I say, "I did not write the tag line."' However, the author did show his support, stating that the tone was definitely fitting for the novel's main character, as he 'found it dark and angry in the same way that Hazel is (at least at times) dark and angry in her humour.' Shailene wasn't so sure. She told *Entertainment Weekly*, 'I had a really strong response to [the tag line],' explaining, 'I could see where [Green] was coming from. But it's still not something that I would have chosen.' She went on to conclude that with the book's ardent fan base, as well as the controversial nature of the film's subject matter, every detail about the film was likely to elicit conflicting positive and negative responses. 'I think that there's so many people who are so passionate about this book that there's nothing that will ever satisfy everyone . . . But it seems like half the people love it and half the people don't like it.' Whichever viewpoint you take, it looked like the project was shaping up to be something edgier and much more interesting than the standard Hollywood romantic drama.

Just over the horizon also lay the possibilities of future *Divergent* sequels. Although a script for *Insurgent*, the first sequel to *Divergent*, had already been commissioned back in May 2013 – it would be written by up-and-coming screenwriter Brian Duffield – and Theo's reprisal of the role of Four was being listed as his next job on his IMDB webpage, in reality, the future of the *Divergent* film franchise was uncertain for most of that year. Confirmation that a sequel had actually been given the go-ahead (pencilled in for a March 2015 release date) came in a roundabout way in late December, when it was announced that Neil Burger would not be returning to direct *Insurgent*. EW.com reported that Summit Entertainment had issued a press release saying, 'Neil Burger is a rock star and he is doing a fantastic job on *Divergent*. We can't wait for you to see the film. But as amazing as Neil is he still cannot be in two places at once and thus needs to finish post-production on *Divergent* while we gear up to start production on *Insurgent*.'

The website spoke directly to Erik Feig, president of production at Lionsgate, who was keen to stress that replacing Burger should not be taken as a reflection of his work on *Divergent*, stating, 'It's the opposite; we're extremely happy with the film Neil has done. He's delivered an amazing, amazing movie, which is really the most important thing. You can't have a franchise without a successful first film. What Neil has done is the hard part: he cast the movie, he created the world and he set the tone.' Burger would complete work on the visual effects and post-production on *Divergent* while, as Feig confirmed, they searched for a new director and continued the pre-production on *Insurgent*, which had by now already begun. When asked if Burger could return for directing duties on *Allegiant*, Feig said, 'You never know ... We're not thinking that far ahead. But one-hundred per cent I will be doing another Neil Burger movie if he wants to.'

While the fate of the *Divergent* sequels looked a lot more secure, it seems likely that even without the franchise, and in as uncertain a profession as acting, Theo and Shailene would not be spending too much time worrying about where the next pay cheques were coming from. A string of recently completed and soon to be released features suggests we should expect to see a lot more of them, be it in the two planned sequels or elsewhere.

Shailene and Theo, like their characters at the end of the first *Divergent* book, are facing a promising future. As Veronica Roth is keen to point out in all her work – you may choose your own destiny, but that one choice can set you on an infinite number of different paths. Anything can happen and nothing is set in stone. It's a universal truth, eloquently presented by Roth. In Tris and Four's case it is the difficult (and dangerous) decision to leave their birth factions and eventually embrace their Divergent nature, while both Shailene and Theo have had to make at least one courageous, life-altering choice in terms of their acting careers. Theo's life changed forever when he finally acknowledged the slowly gestating acting bug and took his place at the Bristol Old Vic. This one decision brought about a complete change in direction, forcing him to channel the raw but unfocused passion and intelligence he effortlessly exudes into something more positive. For Shailene, things may have been very different if she had decided not to skip work in New York and make the cross-country trip to take that fateful second meeting with Alexander Payne in LA that led to her securing her place in *The Descendants*.

While Tris and Four are free to make choices affecting their eventual destinies, they are, for the time being at least, still living powerlessly within an oppressive, tyrannical society. It's safe to say that the thing that sets Shailene and Theo apart from their fictional counterparts, and the thing they have both fiercely fought for, is the freedom afforded them by their success, both in terms of their careers and in their personal lives. Shailene, ever the environmentalist, refuses to take anything for granted and encourages everyone to take a more thoughtful and selfless approach, as she told NextMovie.com, 'You forget that you do choose your life and there are so many things to be grateful for and I feel like society has gotten to that point where we're always looking for the next, and the better, and we lose sight of what's actually in front of us.' In a November 2011 interview with Movieline.com, Shailene had articulately expressed her feelings about the things her career so far had brought her and that she was only too aware that everything in life is uncertain: 'I'm already the most fortunate girl in the world, so I have zero expectations for what the future will bring.'

It's with that in mind that we await the release of the film and, with fingers crossed, eagerly anticipate the chance to re-enter that rich world with planned adaptations of *Insurgent* and, eventually, *Allegiant*. You may have, in reading this book, wanted to find out more about the world of *Divergent* and the real people involved in bringing it to the big screen, yet it is important to remember that ultimately, the fate of the franchise is in our, the viewers, hands. After all, as everyone knows, 'One choice will transform you'.

SOURCES

NEWSPAPERS & MAGAZINES
ASOS
Bello
BlackBook
Boston Phoenix
Chicago Tribune
Coco Eco
Cosmopolitan
New York *Daily News*
Entertainment Weekly
Girls' Life
Glamour
Hollywood Reporter
Impact
The Lab
Los Angeles Times
M
Malibu Magazine
Marie Claire
The New York Times
New York magazine
Newsday
Paper
Pittsburgh Post-Gazette
Rolling Stone
San Francisco Chronicle
Telegraph
Time Out Chicago
Toronto Star
USA Today
Variety
Ventura County Star
W
Wall Street Journal
Washington Post

RADIO
98.1 WOGL – CBS Radio
Here & Now radio show, 90.0 WBUR and NPR
WBEZ 91.5 FM Chicago

ONLINE
411Mania.com
ALA.org/YALSA/teenstopten
Amazon.com
AssignmentX.com
Bestiveread.blogspot.com
Bookish.com
BrodartVibe.wordpress.com
Collider.com
CraveOnline.com
CultBox.co.uk
Deadline.com
E! Online
EW.com
Examiner.com
Goodreads.com
HitFix.com
HollywoodChicago.com
HollywoodCrush.mtv.com
Huffington Post
Hypable.com
Moviefone.com
MoviesOnline.ca
MTV.com
NextMovie.com
NovelNovice.com
PagetoPremiere.com
Screenslam.com
SheReality.com
Teen.com
TheTVChick.com
Totalbookaholic.com
Twitter.com/ShaileneWoodley
Uinterview.com
Upcoming-movies.com
Variety.com
VeronicRothBooks.blogspot.co.uk
WebMD.com
WhatchaReadingNow.com
YAHighway.com
Yahoo! Movies

PICTURE ACKNOWLEDGEMENTS

Page 1: REX / Moviestore Collection (top left); REX / © Warner Bros. / Everett (main picture)

Page 2: Jason Merritt / FilmMagic / Getty Images (top left); REX / © ABC Family / Everett (top right & bottom)

Page 3: REX / Startraks Photo (top left & right); Jason Merritt / Getty Images (bottom)

Page 4: REX / David Fisher (top); Frederick M. Brown / Getty Images (bottom left & right)

Page 5: REX / Moviestore Collection (top); REX / David Fisher (bottom)

Page 6: REX / © FoxSearch / Everett (top & centre); Matt Carr / Getty Images (bottom)

Page 7: REX / © ScreenGems / Everett (top left & bottom); Jeff Kravitz / FilmMagic / Getty Images (top right)

Page 8: Evan Agostini / AP / PA Images (top); Young Hollywood / Getty Images (centre); Alberto E. Rodriguez / Getty Images (bottom)

Page 9: REX / Matt Baron / BEI (left); REX Buzz Foto (right)

Page 10: REX / Startraks Photo (left); Kevin Winter / Getty Images for DGA (right)

Page 11: REX / Giulio Marcocchi / SIPA

Page 12: REX / ITV (top & bottom left); Karwa Tang / Getty Images (bottom right)

Page 13: Larry Busacca / Getty Images (top); Alberto E. Rodriguez / Getty Images (centre & bottom)

Page 14: REX / © CBS / Everett (top); Bobby Bank / WireImage / Getty Images (bottom)

Page 15: Albert L. Ortega / Getty Images (top); Jemal Countess / Getty Images for IFP (bottom)

Page 16: Imeh Akpanudosen / FilmMagic

INDEX